Make a World of Difference

50 Asset-Building Activities to Help Teens Explore Diversity

DAWN C. OPARAH

Search INSTITUTE | *Practical research benefiting children and youth*

KH

Make a World of Difference:
50 Asset-Building Activities to Help Teens Explore Diversity

Dawn C. Oparah

A Search Institute Publication
Copyright © 2006 by Search Institute
Search Institute℠ and Developmental Assets™ are trademarks of Search Institute.

ISBN-13: 978-1-57482-868-9
ISBN-10: 1-57482-868-1

10   9   8   7   6   5   4   3   2   1
Printed on acid-free paper in the United States of America.

Search Institute
615 First Avenue Northeast, Suite 125
Minneapolis, MN 55413
www.search-institute.org
612-376-8955 • 800-888-7828

Credits
Editors: Anitra Budd, Marcie DiPietro Rouman
Book Design: Nancy Wester
Production Coordinator: Mary Ellen Buscher

Library of Congress Cataloging-in-Publication Data
Oparah, Dawn C.
  Make a world of difference : 50 asset-building activities to help teens explore diversity / Dawn C. Oparah.
      p. cm.
  ISBN 1-57482-868-1 (pbk. : alk. paper)
  1. Multicultural education—Activity programs—United States.
  2. Middle school education—Activity programs—United States.
  3. Education, Secondary—Activity programs—United States. I. Title.

LC1099.3.O63 2006
370.117—dc22   2005028437

- "Building Blocks for a Great Life," "Class Acts," "Easy Access," "Faces," Inside Out," "Time of Your Life," and "Who's Here?" are adapted from activities in *More Building Assets Together,* by Rebecca Grothe. Copyright © 2002 by Search Institute.
- "Role Models" is adapted from an activity in *Building Assets Together,* by Jolene L. Roehlkepartain. Copyright © 1997 by Search Institute.
- "That's Sexist!" is adapted from an activity by Jennifer R. Holladay on www.tolerance.org, a Web project of the Southern Poverty Law Center.

About Search Institute
Search Institute is an independent, nonprofit, nonsectarian organization whose mission is to provide leadership, knowledge, and resources to promote healthy children, young people, and communities. The institute collaborates with others to promote long-term organizational and cultural change that supports its mission. For a free information packet, call 800-888-7828.

Licensing and Copyright

Printing Tips
To produce high-quality copies of activity sheets for distribution without spending a lot of money, follow these tips:

- Always copy from the original. Copying from a copy lowers the reproduction quality.
- Make copies more appealing by using brightly colored paper or even colored ink. Quick-print shops often run daily specials on certain colors of ink.
- For variety, consider printing each activity sheet on a different color of paper.
- If you are using more than one activity sheet or an activity sheet that runs more than one page, make two-sided copies.
- Make sure the paper weight is heavy enough (use at least 60-pound offset paper) so that the words don't bleed through (e.g., as often happens with 20-pound paper).

5/2/06

Contents

INTRODUCTION: Exploring Issues of Diversity—The Global Village   **5**

About This Book   **8**

Tips for Facilitators   **11**

SECTION 1:
Personal and Environmental Awareness Activities

1. Building Blocks for a Great Life 15
2. What's the Difference? 18
3. Mixing It Up 21
4. Someone You Know 22
5. Pizza Party 24
6. What's Important to Me? 26
7. Dealing with Prejudice 27
8. In Other Words 29
9. Fear in a Hat 32
10. Social Boundaries 34
11. A New Taste 36
12. Untapped Potential 37
13. Faiths of the World 39
14. Gender Roles 42
15. Different Is Just Different 44
16. Spreading Cultural Goodwill 46
17. Around the World Quiz Bowl 50
18. The Disability Games 53
19. Inside Out 54
20. Diversity Chain 55
21. All Shapes and Sizes 56

SECTION 2:
Skill-Building Activities

22. Media Stereotypes 59
23. Who's Here? 62

24. Challenging My Stereotypes 63
25. Claiming Our Names 66
26. Increasing Our Cultural Competence 68
27. The Civil Rights Movement 70
28. Mental Illness Looks Like 72
29. Remembering Bias 75
30. Time of Your Life 77
31. The Horror of Hate 79
32. That's Sexist! 81
33. On Being Ethnocentric 82
34. Changing Your Race 84
35. Class Acts 86
36. Behind the Labels 87
37. The Effects of "Male Bashing" 88
38. Role Models 89

SECTION 3:
Practice Activities

39. Faces 90
40. Easy Access 91
41. The Grand Mixer 93
42. Entering Your Discomfort Zone 95
43. Cover Stories 96
44. Slogan Contest 97
45. Back in Time 98
46. Mystery Guest 100
47. Taking a Stand 101
48. A Plan of Action 103
49. Say It Loud! 105
50. The Tootsie Roll® Challenge 107

Additional Search Institute Resources 112

Introduction: Exploring Issues of Diversity— The Global Village

On December 26, 2004, a tsunami of enormous size hit Asia and Africa. More than 200,000 people from more than 40 different countries were killed. Many lessons followed, but one stood out: We are all in this world together. When natural disaster or human tragedy strikes, the realization that we all share this world becomes magnified. We see the pain and suffering of others, and it becomes evident that we all belong to one group: humankind. Economic status, gender, skin color, sexual orientation, physical appearance, ability, and age become irrelevant in such times of crisis. Governments and citizens from countries all over the world poured out their love and compassion for the victims of this massive disaster by providing whatever support they could to the survivors. We became united under the shared purpose of providing relief to our suffering brothers and sisters.

The challenge before us is to learn how to live as a global village in the absence of a disaster. Overcoming this challenge begins with sowing seeds of awareness and understanding of the diverse and ever-changing world we live in. Our ability to thrive as a human species depends on our ability to live in unity while living with *diversity*—the many differences in ethnicity, socioeconomic background, sexual orientation, religious practice, appearance, and other characteristics that make up our rich and exciting world.

Why Explore Diversity Issues?

The world our young people will live in as adults will differ vastly from the world of the adults currently educating them. With the click of a mouse, young people can be anywhere in the world. Such instant connection was not the case for most current educators and parents during their own youth. As caring adults, we are therefore charged with training our young people to participate responsibly in a much more global culture. This requires our young people to be aware of and comfortable with the diverse religious practices, genders, ages, ethnicities, appearances, socioeconomic status, sexual orientations, and varying ability levels of all individuals.

All of us, young and old alike, enter society with a store of prior knowledge, closely aligned with our individual and cultural backgrounds, and that knowledge influences how we interact with others. We behave based on how we are raised and, understandably, hold a variety of beliefs and biases about other people. As a facilitator of the activities in this book, you will need to be aware of your own cultural background and biases and let young people know that these cultural influences are common to us all. Facilitators and young people can learn together about different ideas and ways of thinking, with the far-

> All of us, young and old alike, enter society with a store of prior knowledge, closely aligned with our individual and cultural backgrounds, and that knowledge influences how we interact with others.

reaching goal of fostering respect, acceptance, and understanding of those whose lives are not like ours. Although every young person grows up within a cultural context, he or she is shaped over the years by other influences, such as education and social interactions. Education can help young people develop both an awareness of and respect for diversity and cultural differences.

Learning to understand and value differences takes time. It is a comprehensive process that develops like a strong structure—beginning first with a good foundation. Successfully implementing cultural competence and diversity education in a school system or community takes sincere commitment on the part of school administrators, teachers, family members, and community leaders. These decision makers must believe diversity awareness is important for our 21st-century young people, and must demonstrate that belief with strong leadership dedicated to developing an effective education plan. We have a responsibility to provide our young people with the skill sets necessary to become productive, responsible citizens—in their community, nation, and world.

Cultural Competence and Developmental Assets

All of the activities presented here are based on Cultural Competence, Asset 34 of Search Institute's 40 Developmental Assets™. Developmental Assets are the positive qualities, skills, experiences, and opportunities that are critical elements in the healthy development of children and young people. Based on more than four decades of research on human development, these assets paint a picture of the positive things young people need to grow into competent, capable, caring, healthy adults. See page 9 for a complete list of the Developmental Assets.

The 40 assets are divided into eight categories. The first four asset categories focus on external structures, relationships, and activities that create a positive environment for young people:

Support—Young people need to be surrounded by people who love, care for, appreciate, and accept them. They need to know they belong and are not alone.

Empowerment—Young people need to feel valued and valuable. This happens when young people feel safe, when they believe they are liked and respected, and when they contribute to their families and communities.

Boundaries and Expectations—Young people need the positive influence of peers and adults who encourage them to be and do their best. Young people also need clear rules about appropriate behavior, and consistent, reasonable consequences for breaking those rules.

Constructive Use of Time—Young people need opportunities—outside of school—to learn and develop new skills and interests, and to spend enjoyable time interacting with other young people and adults.

The next four categories reflect internal values, skills, and beliefs that young people also need to fully engage with and function in the world around them:

We have a responsibility to provide our young people with the skill sets necessary to become productive, responsible citizens—in their community, nation, and world.

Commitment to Learning—Young people need a variety of learning experiences, including the desire for academic success, a sense of the lasting importance of learning, and a belief in their own abilities.

Positive Values—Young people need to develop strong guiding values or principles, including caring about others, having high standards for personal character, and believing in protecting their own well-being.

Social Competencies—Young people need to develop the skills to interact effectively with others, to make difficult decisions and choices, and to cope with new situations.

Positive Identity—Young people need to believe in their own self-worth, to feel they have control over the things that happen to them, and to have a sense of purpose in life as well as a positive view of the future.

The Power of Assets

On one level, the 40 Developmental Assets represent common wisdom about the kinds of positive experiences and characteristics young people need and deserve. But their value extends further. Surveys of more than 200,000 students in grades 6 through 12 reveal that assets are powerful positive influences on adolescent behavior. Regardless of gender, racial/ethnic background, socioeconomic status, grade in school, type of community, or geographic location, these assets help protect young people from many different problem behaviors. Furthermore, young people who report having more assets are consistently more likely to be successful in school, be leaders, resist danger, maintain good health, value diversity, and demonstrate other indicators of thriving.

About This Book

Make a World of Difference attempts to build understanding and awareness around issues of cultural competence. It is created for use in a community or school setting with young people ages 12 to 18. You can use the activities with stable groups of young people that meet regularly over time, or with migratory populations whose attendance may vary. In a school setting, you can teach these activities as a course or use them to supplement your curriculum. You can also incorporate the activities into after-school programs, leadership programs, juvenile detention centers, in-school suspension programs, faith-based organizations, and community-based organizations.

Each idea in this book provides information about the focus of the activity, materials you will need, suggested time frames, directions on how to conduct the activity, and discussion questions to ask the group at the end of the activity. Each activity touches on three other assets (in addition to Asset 34, Cultural Competence), which are included under "Additional Assets." Sample scripts are also included in **bold** to give facilitators suggestions for speaking to participants. Feel free to adjust these scripts as necessary.

This book is organized into three sections. The activities in section 1, Personal and Environmental Awareness Activities, are intended for people who have very little exposure to and awareness about the issues surrounding each topic. In section 2, Skill-Building Activities, the activities are intended for participants who are beyond the exposure stage and are interested in building skills around a particular topic. Finally, section 3, Practice Activities, gives participants opportunities to try out new, culturally competent methods for expression and relationship building while having the support of group discussions.

How to Use This Activity Book

Although the activities are presented sequentially, you can use whatever activity is appropriate for achieving your intended purpose, as each activity can stand alone. However, for a weekend retreat or intensive training on a particular diversity issue, a number of activities can be combined to create an extended workshop agenda. Most activities can be done in less than an hour.

Before beginning an activity, share the following information with participants to give them a frame of reference for the work you are about to undertake. If the group will meet regularly, you need only read it once:

> **The world around us is changing—fast. We need to be much more prepared than past generations were to be citizens of a diverse, global community. We hope these activities will help us develop our skills as competent global citizens, able to understand many of the issues surrounding diversity and culture. Our goal as a group is to**

40 Developmental Assets™ for Adolescents (Ages 12–18)

Search Institute℠ has identified the following building blocks of healthy development
that help young people grow up healthy, caring, and responsible.

ASSET TYPE	ASSET NAME AND DEFINITION
External Assets	
SUPPORT	1. **Family support**—Family life provides high levels of love and support. 2. **Positive family communication**—Young person and her or his parent(s) communicate positively, and young person is willing to seek advice and counsel from parents. 3. **Other adult relationships**—Young person receives support from three or more nonparent adults. 4. **Caring neighborhood**—Young person experiences caring neighbors. 5. **Caring school climate**—School provides a caring, encouraging environment. 6. **Parent involvement in schooling**—Parent(s) are actively involved in helping young person succeed in school.
EMPOWERMENT	7. **Community values youth**—Young person perceives that adults in the community value youth. 8. **Youth as resources**—Young people are given useful roles in the community. 9. **Service to others**—Young person serves in the community one hour or more per week. 10. **Safety**—Young person feels safe at home, at school, and in the neighborhood.
BOUNDARIES & EXPECTATIONS	11. **Family boundaries**—Family has clear rules and consequences and monitors the young person's whereabouts. 12. **School boundaries**—School provides clear rules and consequences. 13. **Neighborhood boundaries**—Neighbors take responsibility for monitoring young people's behavior. 14. **Adult role models**—Parent(s) and other adults model positive, responsible behavior. 15. **Positive peer influence**—Young person's best friends model responsible behavior. 16. **High expectations**—Both parent(s) and teachers encourage the young person to do well.
CONSTRUCTIVE USE OF TIME	17. **Creative activities**—Young person spends three or more hours per week in lessons or practice in music, theater, or other arts. 18. **Youth programs**—Young person spends three or more hours per week in sports, clubs, or organizations at school and/or in the community. 19. **Religious community**—Young person spends one or more hours per week in activities in a religious institution. 20. **Time at home**—Young person is out with friends "with nothing special to do" two or fewer nights per week.
Internal Assets	
COMMITMENT TO LEARNING	21. **Achievement motivation**—Young person is motivated to do well in school. 22. **School engagement**—Young person is actively engaged in learning. 23. **Homework**—Young person reports doing at least one hour of homework every school day. 24. **Bonding to school**—Young person cares about her or his school. 25. **Reading for pleasure**—Young person reads for pleasure three or more hours per week.
POSITIVE VALUES	26. **Caring**—Young person places high value on helping other people. 27. **Equality and social justice**—Young person places high value on promoting equality and reducing hunger and poverty. 28. **Integrity**—Young person acts on convictions and stands up for her or his beliefs. 29. **Honesty**—Young person "tells the truth even when it is not easy." 30. **Responsibility**—Young person accepts and takes personal responsibility. 31. **Restraint**—Young person believes it is important not to be sexually active or to use alcohol or other drugs.
SOCIAL COMPETENCIES	32. **Planning and decision making**—Young person knows how to plan ahead and make choices. 33. **Interpersonal competence**—Young person has empathy, sensitivity, and friendship skills. 34. **Cultural competence**—Young person has knowledge of and comfort with people of different cultural/racial/ethnic backgrounds. 35. **Resistance skills**—Young person can resist negative peer pressure and dangerous situations. 36. **Peaceful conflict resolution**—Young person seeks to resolve conflict nonviolently.
POSITIVE IDENTITY	37. **Personal power**—Young person feels he or she has control over "things that happen to me." 38. **Self-esteem**—Young person reports having a high self-esteem. 39. **Sense of purpose**—Young person reports that "my life has a purpose." 40. **Positive view of personal future**—Young person is optimistic about her or his personal future.

raise our level of awareness about several diversity issues, while also giving ourselves an opportunity to pause and reflect on our thoughts, feelings, and experiences.

The purpose of these activities is not to promote any particular idea, value, or point of view, but to give us an opportunity to develop greater understanding about the variety of issues surrounding diversity. They are meant to encourage us to be proud of our own cultures and heritages while learning about the cultures of others. In addition, the activities explore issues about diversity that go beyond culture. We will learn about the broad definition of diversity that includes gender, age, religion, race, physical abilities, appearance, sexual orientation, and socioeconomic status. Finally, by participating in these activities, we will accomplish our goals using the positive, supportive lens of the Developmental Assets, the "good things" all young people need to grow up happy, healthy, and responsible.

These activities will help us look at conventions in our communities regarding diversity and cultural competence, examine our own thoughts and feelings, and make the most socially responsible decisions possible. In this way, we will all strive to become more culturally competent as individuals and more positive and productive as a society in general.

After facilitating an activity, it is important to provide participants with some type of closure. During active learning, participants may have had a number of thoughts and feelings they did not have a chance to express. A wind-down or closing segment often allows an opportunity for those expressions. The closing segment can also be an opportunity for the group to summarize the day and receive a thought for reflection or an assignment for the next meeting. Here are some examples of closing statements to ask the group to complete:

- I came in today feeling . . . Right now I am feeling . . .
- Something important I learned today is . . .
- A highlight of the day for me was . . .
- A wish I have as a result of today's activity is . . .
- Something that I will work on doing in the future is . . .

Tips for Facilitators

You do not have to be an expert on diversity issues or on the various cultures of the world to be an effective leader of the activities in this book. You do need some skills as a group facilitator.

Facilitators are special people. They have a good understanding of human nature and group dynamics and know how to use that knowledge to effectively involve participants in active learning exercises. A facilitator is different from a presenter or a teacher. Unlike a presenter, a facilitator says less than the group members. Unlike a teacher, a facilitator is not expected to know everything about the topic. Facilitation is at its best when the participants feel safe in the facilitator's presence but not stifled by it.

A group facilitator plays a number of roles to help the group function effectively and carry out the activity. A facilitator:

- Knows something about the members of the group and why they are participating;

- Understands the purpose and goals of the activities and how to carry them out;

- Checks out the activity space for physical safety;

- Arrives early to make sure the room has been set up properly to conduct the activity;

- Informs the group about the purpose of the activity or exercise beforehand;

- Helps the group set ground rules for emotional safety;

- Keeps the group moving toward the goal at hand;

- Monitors group dynamics and recognizes early warning signs of group dysfunction, including restlessness, sarcasm, and insults;

- Helps ensure group members follow their ground rules;

- Observes how the group is responding to the activity, which helps drive the discussion after the activity;

- Anticipates what might happen in the group and has an alternative plan in case the situation changes;

- Directs and redirects the group through questions to keep the activity on track;

- Addresses inappropriate behavior; and

- Seeks group consensus when appropriate.

> When people know their character won't be attacked, they are more willing to become active, contributing members, able to challenge themselves and to take risks.

Safety

For a group to function at its best, members must feel safe both physically and emotionally. Making the learning environment physically safe and easily accessible to all participants can usually be done without much trouble. Emotional safety is another thing. Even though many activities are done in an atmosphere of fun, the goal is to provide an environment in which participants can challenge themselves, take risks, think critically about topics, and adjust their points of view when appropriate. Therefore, to take risks and be involved in challenging work, participants need to know their dignity will remain intact. They need to know their fellow group members will not pick on them. The group has to be free of put-downs, ridicule, sarcasm, and negative judgment. Participants should feel confident that what they say in the context of the activity and group discussion will stay there, and not be shared with anyone outside the group. When people know their character won't be attacked, they are more willing to become active, contributing members, able to challenge themselves and to take risks. It is through this challenge and risk taking that authentic learning can take place. Setting ground rules can go a long way in providing an emotionally safe environment.

Facilitators have to be careful not to evaluate, validate, or invalidate anyone's opinions or answers.

Ground Rules

Ground rules provide a self-checking mechanism for keeping the participants functioning effectively. They also help develop a group consensus about acceptable and unacceptable behavior. This promotes both physical and emotional safety. *It is important to encourage the group to participate in the development of the ground rules.* The group's participation increases each individual's commitment to the rules and her or his desire to help enforce them. One way to get input from group members is to ask these questions:

- What kind of ground rules do we need to set up so the group doesn't become chaotic?
- What kinds of behavior would make you feel uncomfortable and not want to be a part of the group?
- If this behavior happens, how do you think the group should handle it?

Facilitating Open Discussion

It is important that the facilitator doesn't give her or his opinion but instead remains neutral. When the facilitator shares her or his own opinion early it can slow down or end the discussion because participants are often looking for "right" answers and will assume the facilitator must have the definitive answer on the subject at hand. Facilitators have to be careful not to evaluate, validate, or invalidate anyone's opinions or answers. A good way to respond to comments is through a simple acknowledgment. A simple "Thank you for sharing" or "I appreciate you sharing your thoughts" or "I am glad you were able to explain how you feel to the group" will do, and then the facilitator can move on to the next question or speaker.

Following is a list of sample questions that can either block or aid discussion.

Questions That Block Discussions . . .

- Lead the direction of thought: "Wouldn't it be better if we all could be color-blind?"

- Are closed-ended and seek a one-word reply: "Do you agree with that statement?"

- Are too general or vague: "What do you think about diversity?"

- Embed a question within a question: "Why are you wondering why people can't get along?"

- Assume participants have more experience than they do: "What is the psychological impact of racism over multiple generations?"

Questions That Aid Discussions . . .

- Clarify statements: "What did you mean when you said . . . ?"
- Give participants opportunities to support their statements: "Do you have an example to support what you just said?"
- Encourage participants to go deeper in their thinking: "Could you expand on that idea?"
- Invite participants to join in the discussion: "Jeremiah, what do you think of Justin's response?"
- Engage the entire group: "Has anyone had a similar/different experience?"

Handling Dysfunctional Group Behavior

Once in a while in every group, some behaviors show up that can throw the group off track. The following is a list of typical problem behaviors that can occur, and some recommendations that may aid in an early resolution.

- **Constant laughing or giggling**—Participants can lend a touch of humor to the discussion but don't always know when and where humor is most effective. Accept the break in the discussion and continue using a calm, serious tone of voice. If it persists, at an appropriate break tell the participants you appreciate their senses of humor, then ask them how they think humor interjected at the wrong time affects the group.

- **Lecturing instead of discussing**—Some participants tend to lecture the group as if their opinions were the final word on a subject. Their thoughts are not often relevant to the discussion. Redirect them by saying, "That's a very interesting point. How do you think it relates to [restate the point that was being made]?"

- **Focusing too much on details**—Participants might get stuck on the small details in the discussion and try to pick them apart. ("You said you felt discriminated against last Monday in math, but we only have math on Tuesdays.") Thank them for their corrections and continue with the discussion. If this behavior continues, restate your role as timekeeper and the need to keep the group on task.

- **Withdrawing from the discussion**—Some participants won't say anything, but are obviously thinking a lot about the issue at hand. Call on them if they seem to have something to say rather than waiting for them to volunteer. "Melanie, it looks like you are really giving this question some thought. I am interested in hearing your perspective."

- **Dominating the discussion**—Some participants can start to monopolize the discussion, either by giving long, detailed responses to questions or immediately reacting to another person's contribution with their own opinion. Intentionally call on others who might not be as quick to jump into the discussion. If such behavior continues, at an appropriate break tell these participants you need their help encouraging group members who need more time to articulate their answers: "Before you raise your hand, Devin, please give others a chance to respond to the question first."

- **Pessimism**—Participants may sometimes look for the dark side of every question or issue. They might make statements like, "What's the point of this activity? People will never really be able to understand each other." Rephrase their statements and ask the group if anyone has a different opinion. You can also try relating the topic to their personal interests. ("Valerie, I know you love to ride your skateboard. Have you ever experienced sexism from male skaters?") Participants will often have a harder time being cynical or pessimistic if the discussion connects to them personally.

Section 1: Personal and Environmental Awareness Activities

1 BUILDING BLOCKS FOR A GREAT LIFE

FOCUS: Participants enhance their knowledge of the Developmental Assets.

ADDITIONAL ASSETS: Asset 3, Other Adult Relationships; Asset 15, Positive Peer Influence; and Asset 35, Resistance Skills.

TIME REQUIRED: 45 – 60 minutes.

DIRECTIONS: Before the group meets, cut the photocopy of the Developmental Assets list into 40 strips so that each asset and definition is on a separate strip. Tape one asset and its description to each block. Place the blocks in a pile in the center of your meeting space.

When participants arrive, tell them: **"Each of you has ideas about the good things that young people need in life—about what you need to help you be a caring, responsible, productive member of the community."** Ask youth to call out what they think youth need. Then say: **"This question—What are the good things that children and youth need to be caring, responsible, productive citizens?—is the question behind the work at Search Institute, an organization in Minneapolis, Minnesota. Researchers there have asked over one million young people about their lives to help find an answer. Their answer to this question is a group of experiences and qualities called the Developmental Assets. Many of the things you called out are included in these assets.** (Recall the things participants said that are similar to the assets.) **There are others, too, for a total of 40. One way to think about these assets is that they are building blocks for a great life."**

Ask each participant to pick two blocks from the pile, read both assets silently, and decide which one is stronger in her or his life at this time. Participants keep the blocks that are their strengths and toss the others back into the center. Participants then choose partners and tell each other why they kept the block they did, who in their life helps them to strengthen this asset, and what this person does to build that asset. Repeat this step at least three times, each time choosing a new discussion partner.

Take a few minutes as a group for participants to share who in their lives helps them build assets and tell about things those people do to strengthen their assets.

Share more information about the assets as is appropriate for your group. In-

☑ LIST

You will need:

☐ 40 cubes of the same size (at least four inches) made from small cardboard boxes or upholstery foam.

☐ a copy of the Developmental Assets list (see page 9)

☐ sheets of colored paper (one for each participant)

clude your community's results from Search Institute's *Profiles of Student Life: Attitudes and Behaviors* survey, if the survey was administered in your area.

Ask for a volunteer to represent a fifth-grade student. Point out that even though this young person is trying to build a healthy life, many things in our society work against her or his asset-building efforts. Have the group members name some of the forces and factors that work against them, their friends, and younger kids (such as adults with no time, easy access to drugs, nothing to do after school, negative media, and so on). Give a sheet of the colored paper to each person who responds.

Direct those with papers to wad them up to make "negative snowballs." Tell them to stand behind an imaginary line about five feet from the volunteer "fifth grader" and then throw their snowballs at the volunteer on the count of three. Afterward, ask the volunteer how it felt, and what he or she felt the chances were of avoiding the snowballs.

Ask throwers to retrieve their snowballs and stay in place. Say that the typical number of assets a young person reports experiencing is 19. Remind group members how the Developmental Assets can help protect a young person from negative influences and behaviors. Ask a few participants to work with the volunteer to build a wall with 19 of the asset blocks.

Repeat the snowball throw, noting how many snowballs hit the volunteer this time.

Remind group members of their conversations earlier about the people who have helped them build assets. Point out that a network of positive relationships builds assets. Ask participants to call out the kinds of people the volunteer could have supportive relationships with to reinforce the asset wall (teachers, parents, good friends, coaches, religious leaders, and others). Ask a person representing each type of supportive relationship to come up and stand by the volunteer.

Have youth suggest how these people can be most effective (by listening to the young person, working to stop the snowball throwers, and so on). As suggestions are given, instruct the people up front to act out the directions of the group. Point out how these relationships can help a young person build positive qualities and experiences in life, as well as help protect her or him from risks.

Repeat the snowball toss one last time, with the people representing the volunteer's support system making a wall around her or him. Once again, note how many snowballs hit the volunteer this time.

DISCUSSION QUESTIONS:

1. What will you remember about asset building from this activity?

2. It is never possible to stop all the negative forces (snowballs) that bombard us. When negative forces do reach us, what will happen to a person who has few assets and few people in her or his network?

3. What will happen to a person who has many assets and a strong network?

EDUCATIONAL EXTENSION: At the end of the activity, save the blocks in large boxes or plastic bags. Use them at other gatherings of youth and adults to spark discussion of individual assets and the Developmental Assets framework as a whole. Also, encourage youth to use them when they are teaching younger children about the assets.

② WHAT'S THE DIFFERENCE?

FOCUS: Participants reflect on a time when they felt they did not belong, explore their thoughts and feelings, and examine what they can do to be more inclusive of others who might feel left out and/or unappreciated.

✓ LIST

You will need:

- ☐ a copy of the "What's the Difference?" handout for each participant (see page 20)

- ☐ pencils or pens

- ☐ colored pencils or markers

- ☐ writing paper

- ☐ whiteboard or newsprint and a marker

ADDITIONAL ASSETS: Asset 15, Positive Peer Influence; Asset 33, Interpersonal Competence; and Asset 38, Self-Esteem.

TIME REQUIRED: 20 – 60 minutes.

DIRECTIONS: Distribute a copy of the "What's the Difference?" handout to each participant. Give participants the following instructions:

> **Recall a time in your life when you were with other people and you felt very aware of being different from the rest of the group. Try to remember how you were feeling, what thoughts were in your head, and how you acted. On the left-hand side of the handout, write words or phrases describing how you were feeling, what you were thinking, and what you did. On the right-hand side of the handout, draw a picture of what the situation looked like.**

When they are finished, divide the group into pairs and ask participants to share their answers to each section of the handout with their partner. Give participants at least 10 minutes to complete this step, then bring them back into the larger group. Ask participants the following questions, and record the answers on a whiteboard or newsprint:

1. How did you feel?

2. What did you think?

3. What did you do?

If your group feels comfortable enough, ask if any of the participants would like to share the specific situation that occurred where they felt different.

DISCUSSION QUESTIONS:

1. Looking at the feelings we recorded, are there any common themes about the way people were feeling? If so, what are they?

2. Are there any common themes that connect what you were all thinking? If so, what are they?

3. What does this exercise teach us?

4. What are the implications for us when we are part of a group in which someone else might feel very different from the rest?

5. Should we try to be better about including others in our groups? If yes, what could be some benefits to the group or individual? If there are no benefits, why not?

6. What can we do specifically to be more sensitive to others when they feel left out?

7. What can we do specifically to be better about including others in our groups?

What's the Difference?

Spend a few minutes recalling a time when you felt very different from others. Jot down a few words that highlight or describe the experience, then in a word or short phrase, describe how you felt, what you thought, and what you did. Next, draw a picture that illustrates the experience.

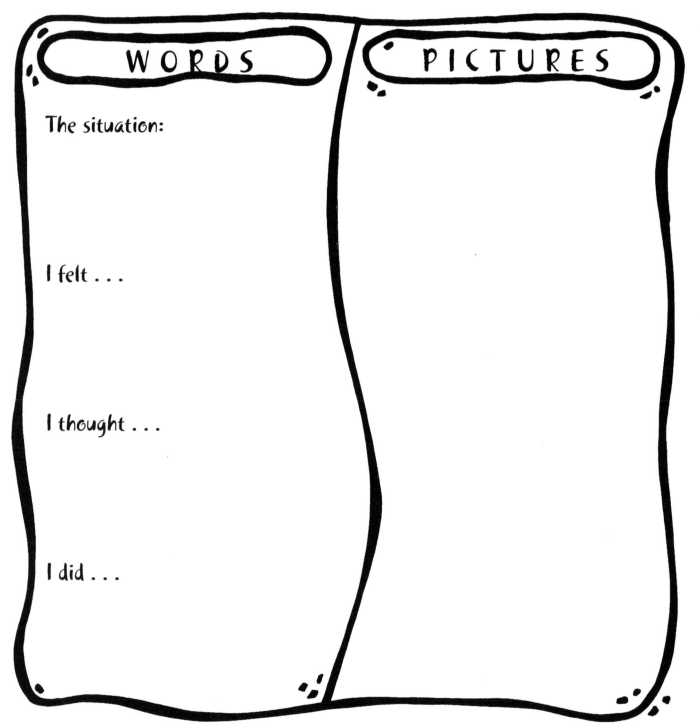

WORDS

The situation:

I felt . . .

I thought . . .

I did . . .

PICTURES

3 MIXING IT UP

FOCUS: Participants take part in a simulation exercise to note that we all have unique preferences and have a right to those preferences.

ADDITIONAL ASSETS: Asset 10, Safety; Asset 33, Interpersonal Competence; and Asset 36, Peaceful Conflict Resolution.

TIME REQUIRED: 25 – 35 minutes.

DIRECTIONS: Before participants arrive, set up a salad bar with the ingredients you've gathered. Tell the participants to make themselves a salad while taking note of the ingredients they use. Once they've made their salads, they should return to their seats. Ask the discussion questions below while the participants eat.

DISCUSSION QUESTIONS:

1. Raise your hand if you put just one item in your salad.
2. Raise your hand if you put three or fewer items in your salad.
3. Five or more? (Teachers can continue this line of questioning to find out the highest number of items a participant used.)
4. Why did you choose some items to put in your salad and not others?
5. Even though each item is different, why do we put them all in our salads?
6. What does the combination of items do for our salads?
7. Does what we choose to put in our salads make them better or worse than anyone else's?
8. If the ingredients represented the diversity in this world, what conclusions could you draw?
9. What would your salad be like if all the items in it tasted the same?
10. Do we have to like every item on the salad bar? Why or why not?
11. Learning to live in a diverse world begins with learning to respect everyone's right to exist, whether we like their politics, belief systems, values, gender, religion, sexual orientation, or ethnicity. What does this statement mean to you?

☑ LIST

You will need:

- ☐ a large bowl for lettuce
- ☐ 20–35 smaller bowls
- ☐ a variety of salad fixings, such as lettuce, chopped carrots, sliced cucumbers, cherry tomatoes, broccoli, red onions, olives, cheese, croutons, bacon bits, hard-boiled eggs, or radishes
- ☐ a variety of salad dressings, such as blue cheese, Italian, French, ranch, or oil and vinegar
- ☐ serving utensils
- ☐ forks and napkins

Note: Participants can contribute the above items, or you can provide them and set them up. If participants are to bring the items, let them know the exact amount based on the number of participants.

EDUCATIONAL EXTENSION: As a take-home assignment, give the participants copies of the following statement and ask them to write one page about their thoughts on the statement, discussing its pros and cons: *The world we live in is not a melting pot where we all are to become one homogeneous being, looking and acting alike. Our world is more like a salad—very heterogeneous, with each ingredient having its own distinct flavor. When we can accept, appreciate, and even celebrate our differences, can we become a world that can live in peace while living with diversity?*

SOMEONE YOU KNOW

FOCUS: Participants learn about the range of feelings aimed at gay, lesbian, bisexual, and transgender (GLBT) people, the risks GLBT individuals take by sharing their sexual orientation with others, and how our personal reactions can be helpful or painful to them.

☑ LIST

You will need:

☐ self-stick notes (three per person)

☐ pencils or pens

☐ whiteboard or newsprint and a marker

ADDITIONAL ASSETS: Asset 10, Safety; Asset 27, Equality and Social Justice; and Asset 33, Interpersonal Competence.

TIME REQUIRED: 20 – 30 minutes.

DIRECTIONS: Share the following information with participants:

Researchers have estimated that at least 10 percent of the population are gay, lesbian, bisexual, or transgender (GLBT). This means that in a room of 30 people, it is statistically likely that 3 people would identify themselves as either gay (men who are sexually attracted to other men), lesbian (women who are sexually attracted to other women), bisexual (people of either gender who are sexually attracted to people of both genders), or transgender (people whose gender identity differs from typical expectations of their physical gender). The likelihood that someone you know is GLBT-identified is high. However, this group of people may remain invisible to you for a number of reasons.

If someone you knew well—a close friend, a cousin, a sibling, or other relative—shared with you that he or she was gay, lesbian, bisexual, or transgender, how would you respond? Write down on separate sticky notes three potential reactions you might have if your best friend told you that he or she was gay, lesbian, bisexual, or transgender. You only have to share what you feel comfortable sharing.

Please note that there may be GLBT participants in the room. It is also very likely that someone in the room has already had the experience of a close friend or relative "coming out," or sharing her or his sexual orientation with them. Remember, don't make any assumptions that we are all the same and share the same experiences in regard to this topic.

When you are done writing, post your notes on the whiteboard [or newsprint]. Read the responses that others have posted.

DISCUSSION QUESTIONS:

1. As you read the different responses on the sticky notes, how did they make you feel? What did they make you think?

2. What kinds of risks do GLBT people take when they choose to reveal their sexual orientation?

3. What is it about society's collective behaviors that might make it difficult for a GLBT person to share her or his sexual orientation?

4. What can we do to make it easier for our friends and relatives to share an important aspect of their lives—their sexual orientation—with us? What are some examples of specific responses we could give if we learned of a friend or relative's sexual orientation?

## 5

PIZZA PARTY

FOCUS: Participants learn about economic class difference by simulating the inequitable distribution of food in the world.

☑ LIST

You will need:

- ☐ bowls for the rice
- ☐ four cups of cooked rice
- ☐ at least two slices of pizza for each participant
- ☐ colored paper
- ☐ scissors
- ☐ money for pizza (ask for $2–$3 per participant in advance, or make alternate arrangements for money)

ADDITIONAL ASSETS: Asset 9, Service to Others; Asset 26, Caring; and Asset 27, Equality and Social Justice.

TIME REQUIRED: 30 – 45 minutes.

DIRECTIONS: Before doing this activity, count the number of participants in your group and divide that number by six. Cut strips of one color of paper equal to one-sixth of the group. Cut strips of a different colored paper so that you have enough strips for the rest of the participants (five-sixths of the group). For example, if you have 24 youth, give 4 of them strips of yellow and give the other 20 strips of green.

In advance, ask the participants to contribute two or three dollars apiece for a pizza party. Order enough so that each participant can have at least two pieces. Be sure to give each participant a strip of paper *before* the pizza is ordered. (Before the pizzas arrive, prepare four cups of cooked rice.)

Have everyone sit together according to the color of their paper strips. Once the pizzas arrive, give all of the pizzas to the smaller group. Give the larger group only rice. Then tell everyone to enjoy their food.

Sit down and talk with the smaller group while ignoring the larger group. (Make sure the group that has the pizza doesn't actually eat more than two pieces each during this time.) Then stop the activity. Let all of the participants eat pizza while going over the discussion questions below.

DISCUSSION QUESTIONS:

1. What was your reaction when you saw how the pizza was being distributed?

2. How did you feel about paying the same amount for a little rice as other people paid for a lot of pizza?

3. How did you feel about having lots of pizza when you knew most people only had a little rice?

4. How did you feel about being treated differently based on how much and what kind of food you had?

5. Analysts have found that one-sixth of the world's population eats most of the world's food while the rest of the world practically starves. What do you think about that?

6. Does this activity have any relevance to your community? Please explain.

7. Are people in our society treated differently based on how many possessions they own, or how much money they have? Please explain.

EDUCATIONAL EXTENSION: To further explore this topic, participants can:

- Research information about the impact of poverty and starvation on children;

- Research local statistics on poverty in their own community;

- Write a paper about the issue; or

- Organize a fund-raiser for poverty at their school. For example, participants can decorate soup bowls and sell them to raise money for a local food shelter.

6

WHAT'S IMPORTANT TO ME?

FOCUS: Participants examine and share their values.

You will need:

- [ ] writing paper
- [ ] pencils or pens
- [ ] discarded magazines and newspapers
- [ ] scissors
- [ ] glue sticks
- [ ] construction paper

ADDITIONAL ASSETS: Asset 38, Personal Power; Asset 39, Sense of Purpose; and Asset 40, Positive View of Personal Future.

TIME REQUIRED: 30 – 45 minutes for making collages; 30–45 minutes for group sharing. *Note: If time is a factor, the individual component of the activity can be given as a follow-up reflection.*

DIRECTIONS: Give participants the following directions:

I want you to make a collage of what is important to you. Included in this collage could be your life's motto, values, principles you live by, quotes that support your personal philosophy, poems that reflect what's important to you, or pictures that help tell a story of your past or future goals and aspirations.

Take a few minutes to write down what is important to you before you start the collage. Look for ways to build your collage around what you have written.

When the participants have completed their collages, ask them to share with the group:

Now that everyone's finished, let's go around the room and share our collages with the group. Each of us will talk briefly about what values or ideas are important to us and how we expressed them in our collages. Important ground rule: For everyone's emotional safety, listen quietly and ask questions only for clarification.

After everyone has shared her or his collage, hold a group discussion.

DISCUSSION QUESTIONS:

1. Why do you think it might be important for us to know what we value and what we stand for?

2. How does knowing what you stand for help in times of confusion?

3. After sharing collages, do any of you feel more connected to people you didn't know well before?

4. Did any themes emerge from the collages? If yes, what were they?

5. How might your collage look if you'd made it five years ago? What about ten years from now?

6. How can you affirm and respect what is important to other people, even if it is not important to you?

DEALING WITH PREJUDICE

FOCUS: Participants examine prejudice and discuss what they can do to positively influence negative situations.

ADDITIONAL ASSETS: Asset 10, Safety; Asset 26, Caring; Asset 29, Honesty; and Asset 36, Peaceful Conflict Resolution.

TIME REQUIRED: 45 – 60 minutes.

DIRECTIONS: Give participants the following instructions:

> **Today we'll be discussing the topics of prejudice and discrimination. Important ground rule: no one is allowed to devalue, justify, or reinterpret another group member's story. If you must comment, then limit your remarks to comments such as: "Thanks for sharing your story," "That must have been difficult," or "I am sorry you had to experience that."**
>
> *(Note: It is important that the group facilitator(s) also share a story.)*

Make the following statements to participants:

- **Anyone can be the target or perpetrator of prejudice or discrimination.**
- **Some people are witnesses to prejudice and discrimination.**
- **People are able to recognize unjust treatment at a very early age.**
- **Prejudice and discrimination do not have to be racial. They can be based on gender, sexual orientation, religion, age, appearance, and other factors.**
- **Prejudice or discriminatory practices do not always happen on purpose or maliciously.**
- **Prejudice and discriminatory practices can be found in school textbooks, the media, and the workplace.**

Divide participants into teams of three to four participants. (Ideally, one facilitator would work with each team.) Once participants are in teams, tell them to recall a time when they witnessed prejudice or discrimination. Participants will have two to three minutes to share their stories with their teams. Participants should state what happened (it is not necessary to mention names), how they felt, and what they did, if anything. Other participants can ask questions for clarification if necessary. Once participants are done sharing their stories, bring them back into the larger group for discussion.

DISCUSSION QUESTIONS:

1. How did it feel sharing your story?
2. Did listening to other people's stories remind you of additional acts of prejudice you may have seen?

3. Did you see common themes among the stories, or common feelings? What were they?

4. We all have prejudices and biases. However, it is how and when we choose to act on them that can be damaging to others. What can we do to minimize the negative impact of prejudices, biases, and discrimination?

5. If you could create a law against prejudice and discrimination, what are some actions, behaviors, or statements you would want to see included?

EDUCATIONAL EXTENSION: Ask participants to write an essay on what they can do to help eliminate prejudices and discriminatory practices from their school, youth group, congregation or community. Have them share their essays at a future group meeting.

IN OTHER WORDS

FOCUS: Participants explore how simply hearing negative statements about groups of people can affect individual behaviors and become better at understanding the power and impact of stereotyping.

ADDITIONAL ASSETS: Asset 28, Integrity; Asset 29, Honesty; and Asset 33, Interpersonal Competence.

TIME REQUIRED: 30 – 45 minutes.

DIRECTIONS: Distribute the "In Other Words" handout facedown. As you do so, tell participants:

> **Please keep your handouts face down as I pass them out. This activity is a free-association exercise. You will silently read a list of words and phrases and then write down the first thought that comes to your mind—without evaluation or censorship. Your answers will be anonymous. Do not write your name or any other identifying marks on this paper. No one will know what you have written, and there are no right or wrong answers.**
>
> **This activity should take less than four minutes. If you see a word or phrase and nothing comes quickly to mind, skip it and go on to the next one. Does anyone have any questions?**

When all the sheets have been passed out, ask the participants to turn them over and begin. After four minutes, ask them to stop and put their pens/pencils down. Collect the sheets and shuffle them well. Tell the participants:

> **I'm going to choose a few of the words and phrases you were given and write down some of the responses. If you see your response listed, there's no need to let anyone else know.**

Choose three or four of the words and phrases listed on the handout and write them on a piece of posted newsprint or a whiteboard. Then, silently go through the participants' completed handouts. Pick several responses for each word and write these down as well. Be sure not to list any participant's name in connection with the responses, whether they're positive or negative. Tell the participants:

> **Look at the responses I've listed. As a group, we're going to decide if the responses are positive, negative, or neutral. Based on what the majority of the group thinks, I'll write signs next to each response—a plus (+) sign if the response is positive, a minus (-) sign if the response is negative, and a zero (0) if the response is neutral or if we're not sure.**

LIST

You will need:

☐ a copy of the "In Other Words" handout for each participant (see page 31)

☐ pencils or pens

☐ whiteboard or newsprint and a marker

☐ a clock, watch, or timer

Once the group has completed this part of the exercise, discuss the following questions.

DISCUSSION QUESTIONS:

1. For the words or phrases we have posted, are there more positive responses or negative responses? Why do you think that is?

2. Where do you think some of the negative responses come from?

3. Does there seem to be a common theme to the responses? If so, where do you think those thoughts and beliefs come from?

4. Are you interested in hearing the written responses to any other words or phrases? (If so, read aloud several of the responses to the word/phrase chosen.) Does there seem to be a common theme to the responses? Please explain.

5. Where does stereotyping come from?

6. How can stereotyping impact our behavior toward others?

7. What are some of the consequences of stereotyping?

8. What can we do as individuals to help minimize the negative impact of stereotyping?

9. What have you learned or observed from doing this activity?

In Other Words

DIRECTIONS: In the blank space next to each word or phrase below, write the first thing that comes to mind. Do not try to write what you think is "right" or politically correct. This is an anonymous exercise, and no one will know how you responded. Please do not place any self-identifying information on this page.

Teen mothers	Senior citizens
Suburbanites	Postal workers
Athletes	Skateboarders
Southerners	Protestants
Reggae music	Homosexuals
Red hair	Police officers
Asians	Brunettes
Pop music	Hearing-impaired people
Mentally ill people	Hip-hop music
Cheerleaders	Buddhists
Native Americans	Latinos
R&B music	College students
Politicians	Trailer-park residents
Caucasians	Classical music
Country music	School administrators
Doctors	African Americans
Foreigners	Rich people
Northerners	Jazz music
Inner-city residents	Hindus
Gifted kids	Jewish people
Heterosexuals	Visually impaired people
Prisoners	Rap music
Lawyers	Europeans
Rural people	Bisexuals
Muslims	Smokers
Blondes	Catholics
Physically disabled people	School dropouts
Poor people	Taxi drivers

The good things you need to succeed in life are called Developmental Assets™. This activity is designed to help you build those assets, especially Asset 34, Cultural Competence.

9 — FEAR IN A HAT

☑ LIST

You will need:

- ☐ newsprint
- ☐ markers
- ☐ self-stick notes
  (10–15 per person)
- ☐ pencils or pens
- ☐ a large hat

FOCUS: Participants learn about hate groups and explore the causes of fear and hate in society.

ADDITIONAL ASSETS: Asset 4, Caring Neighborhood; Asset 10, Safety; and Asset 36, Peaceful Conflict Resolution.

TIME REQUIRED: 45 – 60 minutes.

DIRECTIONS: Share the following information with participants:

- **A hate group is an organization with beliefs or practices that attack or criticize an entire group of people.**

- **In 1998, there were 537 known, active hate groups in the United States. In 2004, there were 751 active hate groups in the U.S.** (Source: "The Year in Hate," The Southern Poverty Law Center [SPLC], *Intelligence Report,* Winter 2000; "Active U.S. Hate Groups in 2004," SPLC, Intelligence Project, 2004.)

- **In 2001 and 2002, 57% of hate crimes recorded by police across Canada were motivated by race or ethnicity; 43% were motivated by religion; 10% were motivated by sexual orientation; and 1% were motivated by disability.** (Source: "Pilot Survey of Hate Crime," the *Statistics Canada Daily,* July 1, 2004. Total equals more than 100% due to multiple motivations.)

- **Hate groups actively target young people as new members and use the Internet as a forum. There were 468 U.S. hate Web sites active in 2004.** (Source: "Hate Group Numbers Up Slightly in 2004," SPLC, *Intelligence Report,* March 2004.)

- **Groups that are often targeted for hate crimes include African Americans, Jews, Muslims, GLBT people, Latinos, foreign-born people, and Native Americans.**

Write the name of each group listed above on a separate piece of newsprint. Ask participants if they know of other groups that are victims of hate crimes in addition to the ones listed. If they name more, write each group's name on an additional sheet of newsprint. Hang the pieces of newsprint around the room.

Read the following quote from Dr. Martin Luther King Jr.:

"People hate each other because they fear each other, people fear each other because they don't know each other, people don't know each other because they have not communicated."

Distribute 10–15 sticky notes to each participant. Ask them:

What do you think the perpetrators of hate fear most about their victims? Write at least one answer to this question for each group. Use

one sticky note per answer. Each sticky note should start this way: "The perpetrator fears _____ about [name of the targeted group]." When you are finished writing, post your answers on the appropriate piece of newsprint.

When all answers have been posted, ask different participants to come up and read the sticky notes. After reading a sticky note, the participant should take it down and put it in the hat. Repeat this until all the sticky notes are in the hat.

Draw only a few sticky notes from the hat and ask participants to brainstorm ways that they think each fear can be minimized or eliminated.

EDUCATIONAL EXTENSION: If this group meets regularly, periodically pull sticky notes from the hat and have the group brainstorm what can be done to minimize each fear. If this group won't meet again, challenge the participants to research hate crimes, hate groups, and the impact both have in the United States and Canada.

DISCUSSION QUESTIONS:

1. Why do you think doing an activity like this might be important to your generation?

2. Was it difficult to come up with the fears that perpetrators of hate might have? Why?

3. What were some of your thoughts and feelings as we did this exercise?

4. Some people say that a great deal of fear comes from ignorance. Do you agree or disagree with this opinion? What are some things we can do individually and collectively to try to eradicate ignorance?

10 — SOCIAL BOUNDARIES

FOCUS: Participants discuss the social boundaries at school and in their community.

☑ LIST

You will need:

☐ a copy of the "Social Boundaries" handout for each participant (see page 35)

☐ pencils or pens

ADDITIONAL ASSETS: Asset 4, Caring Neighborhood; Asset 5, Caring School Climate; and Asset 15, Positive Peer Influence.

TIME REQUIRED: 40 – 50 minutes.

DIRECTIONS: Distribute a copy of the "Social Boundaries" handout to each participant. Have participants write their answers to the questions. When finished, divide the group into three to four smaller teams and have them review their responses to the handout questions with each other. Bring the participants back into the larger group and have each team share highlights of its discussions with the group.

DISCUSSION QUESTIONS:

1 What are some advantages and disadvantages of identifying with a particular group?

2. How do the various groups affect the climate of your school and community?

3. Are there any benefits for people who go beyond their group boundaries? Name them.

4. What are some steps we can take individually and collectively to go beyond our normal group boundaries?

Social Boundaries

1. What are some of the recognizable groups in your school?

2. Would you describe your school as welcoming to all kinds of people or quick to put people into established groups?

3. Do the groups mix together?

4. In your community, what groups get along and what groups do not?

5. How easy is it to move from one group to another? Why?

6. Which group boundaries are the hardest to cross?

7. Many students in the United States say that the cafeteria is where you clearly see social boundaries. Is this true at your school?

8. What would happen if a person from one group attempted to sit with another group in the cafeteria?

9. What social groups are present in your community?

A NEW TASTE

FOCUS: Participants share examples of their cultural heritage.

 LIST

You will need:

☐ an item of cultural significance from each participant

ADDITIONAL ASSETS: Asset 1, Family Support; Asset 19, Religious Community; and Asset 20, Time at Home.

TIME REQUIRED: 45 – 60 minutes.

DIRECTIONS: Ask participants to bring in some food, a piece of clothing, a game, a knickknack, information about a ritual, or something else that represents their cultural heritage. Have participants take turns explaining or demonstrating its cultural significance. (If you have a large group, you many want to form smaller groups for sharing.) For example, a participant of Swedish heritage may bring in an almond and talk about the tradition of hiding the almond in rice pudding (a dessert) before it is served. The person who finds the nut is supposedly the next person to marry and oftentimes receives a small gift as well.

DISCUSSION QUESTIONS:

- What did you enjoy most about doing this assignment on your cultural heritage?
- Did you learn anything that surprised you?
- If you have new feelings about your heritage or another participant's heritage as a result of doing this assignment, please share them.
- Why is it important for people to study and learn about their own heritage?
- Is one person's heritage better than another's? Why or why not?
- How can this exercise help us appreciate and value people from diverse backgrounds?
- Is there anything else we can do to broaden our understanding of our own heritage and that of others?

EDUCATIONAL EXTENSION: Ask participants to interview their parents, grandparents, and other relatives to find out more about their heritage. Encourage participants to look online or in other reference materials for additional information. When young people have collected the information, they should write a one-page report about their findings. Ask participants to state at the end of the paper one reason why they are proud of their heritage. Allow participants to read their papers to the group or post them around the room so others can read them.

UNTAPPED POTENTIAL

FOCUS: Participants explore some of the issues and stereotypes surrounding urban education and young people.

ADDITIONAL ASSETS: Asset 5, Caring School Climate; Asset 16, High Expectations; and Asset 22, School Engagement.

TIME REQUIRED: 45 – 60 minutes.

DIRECTIONS: Divide the participants into two or three smaller teams. Have each team create a short skit that reflects its members' understanding of urban education and "inner-city" kids. Possible scenarios might include a suburban teacher teaching a class of urban students; a group of urban students discussing changes they'd like to make to their school; or a suburban student and an urban student discussing their views on education. Once students have created their skits, have each team perform for the larger group.

Next, distribute the handout with the poem excerpt titled "You Don't Have the Tools to Tap My Untapped Potential." This poem, a commentary on class difference and urban education, is a compilation of quotes taken from interviews with urban youth. Ask participants to read the poem to themselves or take turns reading it aloud. Once participants are finished reading, use the questions below for discussion.

DISCUSSION QUESTIONS:

1. What message do you think the poem is trying to convey?

2. Is this poem relevant to the current education system? Why or why not?

3. What happens to young people who feel the way the speakers feel in the poem?

4. Who are the parties responsible for making this situation better?

5. How do our skits about urban young people relate to the poem and our discussion?

6. How does reading the poem affect your thoughts and feelings about life in urban areas?

You will need:

☐ a copy of the "Untapped Potential" hand-out for each participant (see page 38)

☐ whiteboard or newsprint and a marker

Untapped Potential

An excerpt from "You Don't Have the Tools to Tap My Untapped Potential," compiled from interviews with urban young people by Dawn C. Oparah. © 2001 Amadi Leadership Associates, Inc.

You don't know me.

You don't want to know me.

Yet you think you can teach me.

You come to school with all your degrees thinking you know what it takes to teach me.

You have brought into this classroom all the beliefs and labels about inner-city kids.

We are low-income, deprived, slow learners, behavior-disordered, underachievers, at-risk,
   disadvantaged . . . and the list just goes on and on.

- -

You don't care about me.

You don't know anything about my community.

You don't know who the community leaders are,

You don't know the faith leaders and you have never attended a service on my side of town.

You don't come to community meetings and listen to our issues except maybe an occasional PTA meeting.

You don't know what I like, how I spend my time, or what I want to be when I am older.

You walk around here acting like you know and

You really don't know anything.

- -

If you think I can't, I never will.

If you have low expectations of me, then I will have low expectations of myself.

If you lack the true teaching tools to reach my potential, then I'll become just another statistic.

Thus, my potential remains just that—potential. Potential untapped.

All because you didn't come with the right tools.

- -

If you really want to help me and

Teaching is your calling, not just a paycheck,

You should re-equip your teaching belt with tools that work.

Learn what it takes to teach me and to facilitate my learning.

Bring out my best, learn how to believe in me.

Raise your expectation of my capability.

Don't see only deficits, see my robust assets waiting to explode.

Challenge yourself to learn how to reach and connect with me and students like me—
   "the urban inner-city young people."

- -

Talk to me, study me, try to understand me. Then and only then you might be able to help me,
   teach me and I might even begin to trust you.

The good things you need to succeed in life are called Developmental Assets™. This activity is designed to help you build those assets, especially Asset 34, Cultural Competence.

13 FAITHS OF THE WORLD

☑ LIST

You will need:

☐ a copy of the "Faiths of the World" handout for each participant (see page 40)

☐ "Faiths of the World" answer key for facilitator (see page 41)

☐ pencils or pens

FOCUS: Participants quiz themselves on religions of the world.

ADDITIONAL ASSETS: Asset 9, Service to Others; Asset 19, Religious Community; and Asset 39, Sense of Purpose.

TIME REQUIRED: 30 – 45 minutes.

DIRECTIONS: Ask participants why it might be important to know more about the faiths and beliefs of other people. After listening to their responses, tell them you want to see how much they know about different faiths around the world by taking a quiz.

Distribute the "Faiths of the World Quiz" and ask participants to complete it. After the quiz, ask them how they thought they did, and why. Review the answers with participants.

Faiths of the World

1. What is the most important component of belief in Islam?
   A. Personal sacrifice and fasting
   B. Bowing to the East for prayers five times a day
   C. The Oneness of God (Allah)
   D. Making a pilgrimage to Mecca before death

2. The founder of Buddhism was:
   A. Siddhartha Gautama   B. The Dalai Lama
   C. Tao Te Ching   D. Kahlil Gibran

3. The Qur'an is written in what language?
   A. Hebrew   B. Arabic
   C. Latin   D. Yiddish

4. In the Sikh faith, the word *gutka* means:
   A. Baggy pants   B. A steel band
   C. A small wooden comb   D. A prayer book

5. The main difference between Sephardic and Ashkenazi Jews is:
   A. They descend from different prophets.
   B. They live in different parts of Israel.
   C. They descend from different ethnic groups.
   D. They read different translations of the Torah.

6. How many religious denominations does Christianity include?
   A. 100–200   B. 1,000–1,500
   C. 4,000–5,000   D. Over 9,000

7. Which one is not one of the Five Pillars of Islam?
   A. Prayer (*Salat*)
   B. Pilgrimage (*Hajj*)
   C. Testimony of Faith (*Kalima*)
   D. Righteousness (*Sharia*)

8. Confession, one of the seven sacraments in Catholicism, is also known as:
   A. Acknowledgment   B. Reconciliation
   C. Admission   D. Conference

9. Pagan festivals centered on the spring equinox include all of the following except:
   A. Hallowmas   B. Festival of Trees
   C. Alban Eilir   D. Lady Day

10. In Judaism, what blessing is said over wine to usher in the Sabbath or a holiday?
    A. Kiddush   B. Shavous
    C. Kipa   D. Bracha

11. Quaker congregations are called:
    A. Gatherings   B. Services
    C. Meetings   D. Assemblies

12. The most widely used symbol of Unitarian Universalism is:
    A. The Eternal Sword   B. The Flaming Chalice
    C. The Lily of the Valley D. The New Moon

13. In Hinduism, the Festival of Lights is known as:
    A. Sadhu   B. Choli
    C. Janmashtami   D. Diwali

14. In the Jewish faith, a *mikvah* is used for what purpose?
    A. Healing   B. Protection
    C. Purification   D. Good luck

15. What is the name of the Sikh holy place of worship?
    A. Temple   B. Gurdwara
    C. Shrine   D. Harkrishan

16. *Handfasting* is the Pagan term for a:
    A. Conversion   B. Fast
    C. Prayer   D. Wedding

17. Muslims believe in the existence of Jesus Christ.
    A. True   B. False

18. Taoism, a faith practice that began in the third century BCE, has its roots in which country?
    A. Indonesia   B. Japan
    C. China   D. India

19. The cultivation of virtue is a central tenet of Confucianism. What are two of the major virtues?
    A. Ying and Yang   B. Jen and Li
    C. Chi and Chang   D. Dao and Tao

20. What is the third-largest religion of the world?
    A. Confucianism   B. Buddhism
    C. Hinduism   D. Taoism

The good things you need to succeed in life are called Developmental Assets™. This activity is designed to help you build those assets, especially Asset 34, Cultural Competence.

Faiths of the World: Answer Key

1. What is the most important component of belief in Islam?
C. The Oneness of God (Allah)
This is the foundation of Islam. Muslims only pray to Allah since they believe he is the one true creator of the universe.

2. The founder of Buddhism was: **A. Siddhartha Gautama**
Siddhartha Gautama founded Buddhism during his search for enlightenment. He is also known as the Buddha.

3. The Qur'an is written in what language? **B. Arabic**
The Qur'an is the sacred book of Islam. Muslims believe that the book contains the literal word of God.

4. In the Sikh faith, the word *gutka* means: **D. A prayer book**
In Sikhism, a gutka is a small book containing Sikh daily prayers.

5. The main difference between Sephardic and Ashkenazi Jews is:
C. They descend from different ethnic groups
Ashkenazi Jews come from Eastern Europe, France, and Germany. Sephardic Jews are from Spain, the Middle East, North Africa, and Portugal.

6. How many religious denominations does Christianity include?
D. Over 9,000
While an exact number of Christian denominations isn't available, over 9,000 are included in the World Christian Database.

7. Which one is not one of the Five Pillars of Islam?
D. Righteousness (*Sharia*)
The Five Pillars, or fundamental principles, of Islam are Prayer (*Salat*), Almsgiving (*Zakat*), Pilgrimage (*Hajj*), Testimony of Faith (*Kalima*), and Fasting (*Sawm*).

8. Confession, one of the seven sacraments in Catholicism, is also known as: **B. Reconciliation**
During confession (also known as reconciliation or penance), Catholics meet in private or as a group with a priest to confess their sins and receive absolution.

9. Pagan festivals centered on the spring equinox include all of the following except: **A. Hallowmas**
Hallowmas, sometimes known as All Saints' Day or All Hallows', falls on November 1st. It is a holiday celebrated in Catholic and Anglican churches to honor the saints.

10. In Judaism, what blessings are said over wine to usher in the Sabbath or a holiday? **A. Kiddush**
Kiddush blessings describe the significance of a particular holiday or Sabbath day.

11. Quaker congregations are called: **C. Meetings**
Quaker meetings can take a variety of forms, ranging from structured services led by ministers to open sessions where any participant may speak when moved to do so.

12. The most widely used symbol of Unitarian Universalism is:
B. The Flaming Chalice
Unitarian Universalism accepts members from a wide variety of faiths. Its symbol, the flaming chalice, is a combination of two symbols—the chalice represents sharing, generosity, and love, while the flame symbolizes sacrifice, courage, and illumination.

13. In Hinduism, the Festival of Lights is known as: **D. Diwali**
Diwali is a major Hindu religious festival. It falls in October or November and can last from two to five days. During Diwali, families decorate the inside and outside of their houses with lamps.

14. In the Jewish faith, a *mikvah* is used for what purpose?
C. Purification
A mikvah is a ritual bath used in Jewish ceremonies of physical and spiritual purification, such as the bathing of women following menstruation or childbirth, the dipping of new dishes before use, or as part of a traditional conversion to Judaism.

15. What is the name of the Sikh holy place of worship? **B. Gurdwara**
The Gurdwara contains many rooms, which include Langar room, kitchen, wash areas, cloak and shoe rooms, bedroom for the Guru Granth Sahib, and more.

16. *Handfasting* is the Pagan term for a: **D. Wedding**
In Pagan traditions, handfasting ceremonies are performed to join couples or groups. For some the handfasting is binding for life, while for others it is binding for a year and a day, after which the participants can decide whether or not to renew their commitment.

17. Muslims believe in Jesus Christ. **A. True**
Muslims do not believe Jesus is the son of God or God himself, but they do believe that he was a messenger of God who strove to preach the truth to people.

18. Taoism, a faith practice that began in the third century BCE, has its roots in which country? **C. China**
Taoism is one of the major religions of China, based on the book Tao Te Ching (Classic of Tao and Its Virtue) and the teachings of the philosopher Chuang Tzu. Longevity and immortality are sought by regulating the energies of the body through breathing exercises, meditation, medicinal plants, talismans, and magical formulas.

19. The cultivation of virtue is a central tenet of Confucianism. What are two of the major virtues? **B. Jen and Li**
Jen: a benevolent and humanitarian attitude.
Li: maintaining proper relationships and rituals that enhance the life of the individual, the family, and the state.

20. What is the third-largest religion of the world? **C. Hinduism**
Hinduism currently has roughly 900 million followers around the world. Hinduism is a *henotheistic* religion—one that recognizes a single deity, but recognizes other gods and goddesses as facets, forms, or manifestations of that deity.

The good things young people need to succeed in life are called Developmental Assets™. This activity is designed to help you build those assets, especially Asset 34, Cultural Competence.

GENDER ROLES

FOCUS: Participants imagine what being a member of the opposite gender might mean.

☑ LIST

You will need:

☐ writing paper

☐ pencils or pens

ADDITIONAL ASSETS: Asset 15, Positive Peer Influence; Asset 16, High Expectations; and Asset 27, Equality and Social Justice.

TIME REQUIRED: 30 – 45 minutes.

DIRECTIONS: Tell participants:

> I want you to pretend that tomorrow you will switch genders. All the females will become males and all the males will become females. As I read the following questions, imagine how your life will be different in the opposite gender role and jot down your responses on a piece of paper. Remember, this activity is meant to open a positive dialogue about gender. Please don't use it to criticize or dismiss the opposite sex.

1. When you wake up tomorrow, will you do anything differently?
2. How will your parents treat you? Will it be the same or different?
3. When you go to school, how will your peers treat you?
4. Will your teachers treat you differently?
5. What will your activities after school be like?
6. Are you seen as more able or less able in your new gender role?
7. Does anyone make any negative comments to you about your gender?
8. Do you still have the same friends?
9. What are your goals for the future in your new gender?
10. Do you feel more or less safe in your new gender role?
11. How do you treat your family? friends? strangers?

After reading these questions, ask participants (individually or in pairs) to act out their responses in front of the group. For instance, participants can act out how their morning routine would change, how their peers would treat them, or what their after-school activities would be in their new gender roles.

DISCUSSION QUESTIONS:

1. How easy or difficult was it to imagine yourself as a member of the opposite gender?
2. What do you imagine would be easy about being a member of the opposite gender? Why?

3. What do you imagine would be difficult about being a member of the opposite gender? Why?

4. Did you have any new insights or appreciations for the opposite gender?

5. Did you feel more privileged or less privileged in your new gender role?

6. What are some of the advantages the other gender has that you don't?

7. What are some disadvantages the other gender has that you don't?

8. How can this help us in our appreciation of the opposite gender?

9. After sharing this activity and discussion, how accurate do you think your perceptions of the opposite gender were?

10. Will you change any part of your behavior as a result of this activity? How?

15 DIFFERENT IS JUST DIFFERENT

FOCUS: Participants understand how diverse people can be.

 LIST

You will need:

☐ five large signs posted in the room labeled STRONGLY AGREE, AGREE, DISAGREE, STRONGLY DISAGREE, and INDIFFERENT

ADDITIONAL ASSETS: Asset 28, Integrity; Asset 29, Honesty; and Asset 35, Resistance Skills.

TIME REQUIRED: 30 – 45 minutes.

DIRECTIONS: Tell participants the following:

I'm going to read some statements aloud to you. Stand by the sign that most closely reflects your opinion on the statement.

Read a number of the statements and ask participants to notice the makeup of the group every time they move.

1. I like guacamole.
2. I'd rather go to the beach than the mountains.
3. I think marijuana should be legalized.
4. I like to run on a regular basis.
5. I enjoy hunting and/or fishing.
6. My favorite kind of movie is romance.
7. I think people should go to marriage counseling before getting married.
8. I can take a stand about what I believe.
9. I think cultural differences should be valued.
10. I enjoy being alone.
11. I enjoy reading.
12. I like video games.
13. I love to dance.
14. I like going to sporting events.
15. I believe smoking is wrong, even when it's legal.
16. I like roller coasters.
17. Exercise is very important to me.
18. Animal rights are important to me.
19. I like dogs.
20. I like camping outdoors.
21. I like surprises.
22. I like to play board games.
23. I believe helping people is unproductive; people should learn to help themselves.

24. I like to babysit.

25. I think everyone should play a musical instrument.

26. I like spending time with my parents.

27. I like Chinese food.

28. I like to talk on the phone.

29. I think people can't be successful unless they go to college.

30. I think it's important to love my country.

DISCUSSION QUESTIONS:

1. Were you ever in a group where you felt like the minority? How did that make you feel?

2. Would people know the "real you" if they knew your responses to all of the statements we just reviewed? Why or why not?

3. Do we all need to feel the same way about everything? Why or why not?

4. Does being different change your value or self-worth? Why or why not?

5. What are the advantages and disadvantages of people having different feelings and thoughts about some issues?

16

SPREADING CULTURAL GOODWILL

FOCUS: Participants simulate mingling with people whose cultural norms, customs, and behavior are different from their own.

ADDITIONAL ASSETS: Asset 4, Caring Neighborhood; Asset 33, Interpersonal Competence; and Asset 36, Peaceful Conflict Resolution.

TIME REQUIRED: 30 – 60 minutes.

DIRECTIONS: Divide the group in half, taking care to ensure there is a balanced number of males and females in both groups. If you have more of one gender than the other, ask some people to "play" the opposite gender (signify this by having the participants who are trading gender roles cut their stickers in half before placing them on their foreheads).

After dividing the group in half, take one of the two groups out of the main room or meeting area. Give each person in this group a copy of the "Baird Culture" handout and enough blue stickers so that each participant can place one on her or his forehead. Ask them to read about their new roles as members of the Baird culture.

Meanwhile, return to the main room or meeting area and distribute the "Walda Culture" handout to the remainder of the participants, with enough green stickers so that each participant can place one on her or his forehead. Review their roles with them and have participants practice them briefly.

Return to the Baird group and review their roles with them; have them practice briefly and ask if they have any questions. Make sure both groups know that once they are brought together again, they must stay in their new roles and are not allowed to tell members of the other group about their cultural norms. As the Baird group reenters the main room, announce to the participants:

Welcome! You have been invited to this special gathering for the purpose of spreading goodwill to people of different cultures. Since cultural goodwill starts with communication, I invite you to help yourself to refreshments, enjoy the music, and most of all, please get to know one another. Let the cultural goodwill begin!

Start the music and allow the two groups to mingle for about 10 minutes or so. You can shorten the time if the participants begin to polarize into their own cultural groups. As the facilitator, mingle and observe what is happening and listen to some of the comments that are being made. When it is clear that participants from the Baird culture have met almost everyone, stop the music and ask the entire group to return to their seats.

DISCUSSION QUESTIONS:

1. Members of the Baird culture, give me some words or short phrases to describe the people wearing green stickers. (Record their answers.)

2. Members of the Walda culture, give me some words or short phrases to describe the people wearing blue stickers. (Record their answers on newsprint.)

3. Members of the Baird culture, if you were given a chance to spend a whole day with the people wearing green stickers, would you want to do it?

4. Members of the Walda culture, if you were given a chance to spend a whole day with the people wearing blue stickers, would you want to do it?

5. Share some of the thoughts and feelings you had as you were interacting in the simulation. (As the facilitator, you may share some of the observations you made during the simulation.)

6. Look at the words and phrases that were used to describe the two groups. What do you notice?

7. Why is it that we tend to look at people who are different from us through a generally negative lens?

8. Did members of the same group begin to retreat back to their own culture after a while?

9. How would you explain the phrase "staying in your comfort zone"? What are some examples from your own life of "staying in your comfort zone"?

10. Why is it difficult to come out of our comfort zones and interact with people who appear to be very different from us?

11. What might happen if, the next time you went to the cafeteria or got on the bus, you asked if you could sit with a group you don't normally sit with?

12. When people's customs are different from our own, what are some positive ways in which we can respond?

The Baird Culture

Below are customs of the Baird people:

- **Baird people are informal and friendly.**

- **Among the Baird, there is no gender discrimination. Men and women behave the same way.**

- **Baird people are outgoing. They love to meet people, especially people from different places.**

- **They normally extend their hand for a handshake when meeting someone new.**

- **Baird people usually make contacts that are brief but very friendly.**

- **Baird people become familiar quickly and call everyone by their first name.**

- **Baird people value contact with the opposite gender more than contact with the same gender.**

The good things you need to succeed in life are called Developmental Assets™. This activity is designed to help you build those assets, especially Asset 34, Cultural Competence.

The Walda Culture

Below are customs of the Walda people:

- **Waldas are generally self-contained. They prefer to engage in conversation with members of their own culture. They don't initiate conversations with others, but will speak when spoken to.**

- **Waldas are generally formal in their interactions with others, addressing others as "my lady" and "my lord" as a sign of respect. They generally don't call others by their first name.**

- **When away from their cultural setting, Walda men must be chaperoned by Walda women.**

- **In the Walda culture, men are considered the weaker gender. They are forbidden to make eye contact with women who are not members of their own culture.**

- **Walda men cannot talk directly to foreign women. They can only respond through their female chaperones.**

- **Walda men can make eye contact with and talk to foreign men.**

17 AROUND THE WORLD QUIZ BOWL

FOCUS: Participants assess their cultural knowledge of the world and historical contributions by North Americans from a variety of cultural backgrounds.

☑ LIST

You will need:

- ☐ a copy of the "Around the World Quiz Bowl" handout for each of five or six teams (see page 51)

- ☐ "Around the World Quiz Bowl" answer key for facilitator (see page 52)

- ☐ a world atlas or map for facilitator

- ☐ a set of encyclopedias or Internet access for facilitator

- ☐ several small prizes (small notepads, stickers, temporary tattoos, movie passes, candy, and so on)

- ☐ pencils or pens

ADDITIONAL ASSETS: Asset 14, Adult Role Models; Asset 22, School Engagement; and Asset 25, Reading for Pleasure.

TIME REQUIRED: 30 – 45 minutes.

DIRECTIONS: Divide the participants into five or six smaller teams. Distribute a copy of the quiz to each team, asking participants to work with their team members to answer as many questions as possible. Participants should guess any answers they're unsure of. Allow about 10 minutes for the teams to complete the quiz. Afterward, review the answers with the participants, awarding one point for each correct answer. You can record each team's score on the back of your quiz answer key. Once you've reviewed all of the answers, tally each team's score and announce the winning team. Award prizes to participants on the winning team.

DISCUSSION QUESTIONS:

1. How many of you think you did well on the quiz? (If very few raise their hands, ask the participants why they think they didn't do well.)

2. When naming famous North Americans and their contributions, if you eliminate the answers that represent dead people, athletes, and entertainers, would you still have people on your list?

3. Why might it be important for us to know more about the world? How does that benefit us?

4. Why do you think we know so little about contributions of North Americans from a variety of ethnic and racial backgrounds?

5. What can we do to become more aware of the world and people of cultures different from our own?

6. What have you learned from taking this quiz?

Around the World Quiz Bowl

1. **How many countries are in the world?**

2. **How many countries are in North America?**

3. **How many countries are in South America?**

4. **How many countries are in Europe?**

5. **How many countries are in Asia?**

6. **How many countries are in Africa?**

7. **How many countries are in Australia/Oceania?**

8. **Name 12 African countries.**

9. **Name 12 Asian countries.**

10. **Name 5 famous North Americans of African descent and their historical contributions.**

11. **Name 5 famous North Americans of Asian descent and their historical contributions.**

12. **Name 5 famous Native North Americans and their historical contributions.**

13. **Name 5 famous North Americans of Hispanic/Latino descent and their historical contributions.**

14. **Name 5 famous North Americans of European descent and their historical contributions.**

Around the World Quiz Bowl: Answer Key

1. How many countries are in the world? **192 (according to the Central Intelligence Agency's 2005 World Factbook)**
2. How many countries are in North America? **23**
3. How many countries are in South America? **12**
4. How many countries are in Europe? **46**
5. How many countries are in Asia? **44**
6. How many countries are in Africa? **53**
7. How many countries are in Australia/Oceania? **14**

Note: Use an atlas or map to verify responses to the next two questions.

8. Name 12 African countries.
9. Name 12 Asian countries.

Note: Use encyclopedias or the Internet to verify responses to the next five questions. Two popular online encyclopedias are the Encyclopedia Britannica (www.britannica.com) and Encarta (encarta.msn.com).

10. Name 5 famous North Americans of African descent and their contributions.
11. Name 5 famous North Americans of Asian descent and their contributions.
12. Name 5 famous Native North Americans and their contributions.
13. Name 5 famous North Americans of Hispanic/Latino descent and their contributions.
14. Name 5 famous North Americans of European descent and their contributions.

THE DISABILITY GAMES

FOCUS: Participants simulate having a physical disability and brainstorm ways to make physical activities more inclusive.

ADDITIONAL ASSETS: Asset 9, Service to Others; Asset 27, Equality and Social Justice; and Asset 33, Interpersonal Competence.

TIME REQUIRED: 45 – 60 minutes.

DIRECTIONS: Help participants "put on" various disabilities using scarves, eye patches, ear plugs, or heavy socks. For example, you can use scarves to

- Tie participants' arms in slings (simulating amputation or paralysis);
- Blindfold participants (simulating blindness);
- Cover participants' mouths (simulating muteness); or
- Tie a filled, heavy sock to participants' arms or legs (simulating partial paralysis).

Once participants are "wearing" their disabilities, divide them into four or five teams. Give each team a piece of recreation or sports equipment and have teams play a game (in separate parts of the play area) for 15–20 minutes. If time is available, rotate the equipment so that each team has a chance to try playing a different game.

When participants have completed this step, have them remove their "disabilities" but remain in their teams. Give each team a piece of newsprint and a marker. Have members brainstorm and list ways the game(s) they played could be more inclusive of all levels and types of physical ability. Have each team share one or two of its ideas with the larger group, and then go over the following discussion questions.

LIST

You will need:

- [ ] an open play area, such as a gym or field
- [ ] recreation and sports equipment, such as rubber balls, soccer balls, jump ropes, tennis rackets, and hula hoops
- [ ] large scarves
- [ ] eye patches or sleep masks
- [ ] ear plugs
- [ ] socks filled with a heavy substance, such as sand, coins, pebbles, or salt
- [ ] newsprint
- [ ] markers

Note: If possible, one or two wheelchairs would be helpful for this activity.

DISCUSSION QUESTIONS:

1. How did the disability you "wore" change how you participated in the games?
2. Was every person on your team able to participate in the games you played? If not, what did you do about it?
3. Did other participants treat or talk to you differently based on your disability? Please explain.
4. Did you ever have to ask another participant for help during the games? If so, how did that make you feel?
5. What strengths might someone develop as a result of having these various disabilities?
6. What physical activities can we think of that anyone could participate in, no matter what her or his level or type of ability?

INSIDE OUT

FOCUS: Participants share their experiences of being included and excluded.

ADDITIONAL ASSETS: Asset 4, Caring Neighborhood; Asset 5, Caring School Climate; and Asset 7, Community Values Youth.

TIME REQUIRED: 30 – 45 minutes.

DIRECTIONS: Before the activity, place chairs in a circle, with room to walk between each one.

Invite participants to sit in the circle of chairs. Explain that you will read a statement and that their job is to listen, think, and then follow the instructions.

Pause for a few moments after each statement to allow participants time to respond and notice where various participants are standing. Use these statements, adjusting them as appropriate for your group:

- **If you ever have felt that you were being treated unfairly because of your gender, stand outside the circle;**
- **If you ever have felt welcomed by a group of people you didn't know, stand inside the circle.**
- **If you ever have felt afraid for your safety because of your race, stand outside the circle.**
- **If you have a friend who has a different cultural, racial, or ethnic background, stand inside the circle.**
- **If you speak more than one language, stand inside the circle.**
- **If you ever have felt that you were being treated unfairly because of your accent or language, stand outside the circle.**
- **If you ever have felt that you were being treated unfairly because of the shape or size of your body, stand outside the circle.**
- **If you ever have felt embarrassed by the way your parents look, speak, or act, stand outside the circle.**
- **If you ever have introduced yourself to someone you didn't know, stand inside the circle.**

After you've finished reading the statements, stay in the circle and discuss the following questions.

DISCUSSION QUESTIONS:

1. What surprised you about this activity? Did anything make you feel uncomfortable or sad? If so, what?

2. How does this activity mirror what can happen in school and in our communities in general?

3. Why is it easier sometimes to think about people's differences rather than their similarities?

☑ **LIST**

You will need:

☐ one chair for each participant

DIVERSITY CHAIN

FOCUS: Participants claim their diverse qualities while acknowledging their similarities to other members of the group.

☑ LIST

You will need:

- ☐ 1" x 8" strips of construction paper (five per participant)
- ☐ tape or glue
- ☐ markers

ADDITIONAL ASSETS: Asset 8, Youth as Resources; Asset 37, Personal Power; and Asset 39, Sense of Purpose.

TIME REQUIRED: 30 – 40 minutes.

DIRECTIONS: Hand out five strips of construction paper to each participant. Ask them to think about five things that make them different from other members of the group. These five things might include a philosophy, belief, characteristic, special gift or talent, rare medical condition, background, aspiration for the future, or unusual accomplishment. Once the participants have had a chance to reflect, ask them to write down the five things they chose, one on each strip of construction paper.

Next, ask the participants to think about five things that make them similar to other members of the group, and to write them on the back of each strip of construction paper.

When the participants are finished writing, go around the room and ask them to share their five similarities to the group. Go around again and ask them to share the five things that make them different from the group. (If you have a large group and very little time, you may ask the participants to read only two or three.)

Go over the discussion questions with the group. Afterward, have the participants tape or glue their strips of construction paper into links to form a long chain. This chain can then be displayed or recycled as necessary.

DISCUSSION QUESTIONS:

1. Why is diversity important?
2. Why do some people fight against diversity?
3. How did it feel sharing the qualities that make you different from the group?
4. Is it important to you to have your diverse qualities valued by others? Why or why not?
5. Each of the links on our chain is different, yet they all connect with each other to make a single chain. Does this have any relevance for how we think about diversity? Please explain your answer.

FOCUS: Participants learn about the emphasis society places on young people to look a certain way and the impact that expectation has on their behavior and self-image.

☑ LIST

You will need:

- ☐ discarded lifestyle, fashion, and/or fitness magazines (one for each participant)

- ☐ large signs posted in the room labeled TRUE and FALSE

- ☐ a tally sheet for each participant (see page 58)

ADDITIONAL ASSETS: Asset 37, Personal Power; Asset 38, Self-Esteem; and Asset 40, Positive View of Personal Future.

TIME REQUIRED: 45 – 60 minutes.

DIRECTIONS: Tell the participants you want them to research the emphasis the print media place on beauty and dieting. Give each participant a magazine and tally sheet and ask them to tally the results for their magazine. Give them about 15 minutes to complete this task.

Next, divide the participants into smaller teams and ask them to share their findings with each other. Once the teams have had time for discussion, ask each team to share three to four conclusions from its findings with the larger group.

Share the following statements with the participants. Ask them to stand by the sign (TRUE or FALSE) they believe is correct. Participants should be prepared to explain why they chose their answers.

- **90% of people with eating disorders are girls between the ages of 12 and 15. [TRUE]** (Source: The Center for Mental Health Services.)
- **335,000 people 18 years and younger had plastic surgery in 2003. [TRUE]**
  (Source: The American Society of Plastic Surgeons.)
- **1% of people with anorexia or bulimia are male. [FALSE]**
  (According to the Anorexia Nervosa and Related Eating Disorders, Inc., an estimated 10% of people with anorexia are male.)
- **70% of women and 35% of men are dieting at any given time. [TRUE]**
  (Source: The National Eating Disorder Information Centre.)
- **In a 1986 study of almost five hundred 10-year-old girls, 16% reported that they had dieted at least once. [FALSE]** (In actuality, 81% of the 10-year-old girls in the study reported dieting at least once. Source: Mellin, Scully & Irwin, 1986.)
- **Over 70 million people worldwide are affected by eating disorders. [TRUE]** (Source: The Alliance of Eating Disorders Awareness.)

DISCUSSION QUESTIONS:

1. How does the magazine research you conducted today relate to some of the statements we read?

2. Most magazines target a very specific audience, which affects the kinds of messages they send to their readers. Think about what audience your magazine was trying to reach. What specific messages about body image was your magazine trying to send to its intended audience?

3. The message that you must be thin, or else feel guilty and ashamed if you are not, can be pervasive in society. What impact does that message have on young people?

4. Do males and females receive different messages from society concerning body image? What about people from different ethnic backgrounds? If so, how are the messages for different groups of people different? How are they similar?

5. In general, how does society treat people who are overweight?

6. What can be done to help people feel good about who they are, regardless of their shape or size?

7. If you could write a message to the editors and owners of these magazines, what would you tell them?

8. When people don't feel good about the way they look, how does that affect their self-esteem?

9. What positive messages can we tell ourselves and others to counterbalance negative messages about body image?

Magazine Tally Sheets

Name of Magazine _____ **Target Audience** _____ **Target Age**_____

# of pages _____   # of Feature Articles _____   Date of Issue _____

# of Advertisements about Beauty & Beauty Aids	
# of Advertisements about Dieting/Getting in Shape	
# of Advertisements about Clothes & Accessories	
# of Articles about Beauty and Beauty Aids	
# of Articles about Dieting/Getting in Shape	
# of Articles about Clothes & Accessories	
# of Articles about Career and Work	

Name of Magazine _____ **Target Audience** _____ **Target Age**_____

# of pages _____   # of Feature Articles _____   Date of Issue _____

# of Advertisements about Beauty & Beauty Aids	
# of Advertisements about Dieting/Getting in Shape	
# of Advertisements about Clothes & Accessories	
# of Articles about Beauty and Beauty Aids	
# of Articles about Dieting/Getting in Shape	
# of Articles about Clothes & Accessories	
# of Articles about Career and Work	

Name of Magazine _____ **Target Audience** _____ **Target Age**_____

# of pages _____   # of Feature Articles _____   Date of Issue _____

# of Advertisements about Beauty & Beauty Aids	
# of Advertisements about Dieting/Getting in Shape	
# of Advertisements about Clothes & Accessories	
# of Articles about Beauty and Beauty Aids	
# of Articles about Dieting/Getting in Shape	
# of Articles about Clothes & Accessories	
# of Articles about Career and Work	

Section 2: Skill-Building Activities

22 — MEDIA STEREOTYPES

FOCUS: Participants become active observers to learn how the media reinforce stereotypes.

✓ LIST

You will need:

☐ a copy of the "Media Stereotypes Log" for each participant (see page 61)

☐ a dictionary

☐ index cards

ADDITIONAL ASSETS: Asset 28, Integrity; Asset 37, Personal Power; and Asset 38, Self-Esteem.

TIME REQUIRED: One 15– to 20–minute meeting and one 30– to 45–minute meeting over two weeks.

DIRECTIONS: Before the activity, use a dictionary to write down the definition of "stereotype" on an index card.

When participants arrive, divide them into four or five teams and give each team an index card. Ask them to take two to three minutes to define the word "stereotype" in their teams and write their answers on the index cards. Participants should also write their initials on the back of their team's index card.

After they've completed this step, collect the index cards and shuffle them together, making sure to include the index card with the dictionary definition you wrote down earlier. Read the definitions aloud and have participants vote on which one they believe is the correct definition. Once participants have voted, share the correct definition with the group and ask them to give any examples of stereotypes they've witnessed, either in person or in the media.

Next, give the following instructions to the group:

For the next two weeks, I would like you to become the Media Stereotype Police. Observe stereotypes in a variety of different media, including television, radio, newspapers, magazines, and advertising.

Give each participant a copy of the "Media Stereotypes Log" handout. Tell them:

It is very important for you to completely fill out the stereotypes log, especially your thoughts and the descriptions of the stereotypes you observed.

Provide a reminder to participants at the one-week mark. After two weeks, collect the logs. Have a group discussion about the participants' findings and what they found particularly interesting or disturbing.

DISCUSSION QUESTIONS:

1. Did any particular stereotypes seem to occur frequently?

2. Did certain groups seem to be stereotyped more frequently than others?

3. Where did you tend to notice the most stereotypes? the least?

4. Were there any stereotypes you found particularly disturbing? Why?

5. When you noticed stereotypes, what purpose do you think they were meant to serve?

6. How can we become more aware of stereotypes and oppose them when we see them?

Media Stereotypes Log

During the next two weeks, observe the stereotypes you find in television programs, commercials, radio, news, movies, magazines, and newspapers. Consider the following questions to help guide you in your observations:

- What makes you notice the stereotype?
- How do the media help reinforce the stereotype?
- How do the media use language, dialect, and accents to promote stereotyping?
- Do you see some groups more stereotyped than others?
- Are there groups that are not stereotyped in the media?

Date	Type of Media	Group Being Stereotyped	Description of Stereotype	Your Thoughts

The good things you need to succeed in life are called Developmental Assets™. This activity is designed to help you build those assets, especially Asset 34, Cultural Competence.

WHO'S HERE?

FOCUS: Participants investigate the socioeconomic demographics of their community.

☑ LIST

You will need:

☐ demographic data for your community (Census data are available from your city, county, township office, or library reference desk. United States Census information is available at www.census.gov. The link to "State and County Quick Facts" is especially helpful.)

☐ markers

☐ newsprint

☐ reference materials or Internet access

ADDITIONAL ASSETS: Asset 4, Caring Neighborhood; Asset 9, Service to Others; and Asset 27, Equality and Social Justice.

TIME REQUIRED: 45 – 60 minutes. *Note: This activity may take more than one session*

DIRECTIONS: Before the activity, make copies of current, local census data for youth to review. Include any available information about income, poverty, education, job growth (or loss), home ownership, household size, and literacy in your community or neighborhood. If possible, bring these data for 30 and 50 years ago as well. If you would like to expand this activity, invite a person who works with impoverished people in your community to talk about services your community provides to people living in poverty and to answer questions.

Allow time for participants to look individually through the census data you have provided. As a group, discuss interesting or surprising information they discovered.

Compare the current information about socioeconomic changes with the data from 30 and 50 years ago. Ask participants to offer their theories about why these changes took place.

Divide the participants into teams of three. Ask each team to research one aspect of the socioeconomic demographics of your community and record five key pieces of information about it on newsprint to share with the group. For example, participants may research literacy issues and list organizations that work to promote it in your community. Provide reference books or access to the Internet. Allow 15 minutes for teams to work. Ask each team to present its five key pieces of information, and then discuss the following questions.

DISCUSSION QUESTIONS:

1. Can you think of other ways to learn more about the different members of our community?

2. Do you know anyone from a socioeconomic bracket that is different from yours (for instance, you consider yourself middle-class and have a friend who is quite wealthy)? If so, how did you meet each other? What do you have in common? What has been challenging about getting to know each other?

3. What different reactions to impoverished residents in your community have you observed in other adults and young people? Which reactions seem helpful? Which seem to cause problems? Why do you suppose people respond to impoverished people in the ways they do?

24 CHALLENGING MY STEREOTYPES

FOCUS: Participants learn about the role they can play in recognizing and minimizing stereotyping by taking personal responsibility for their own behavior.

ADDITIONAL ASSETS: Asset 8, Youth as Resources; Asset 28, Integrity; and Asset 30, Responsibility.

TIME REQUIRED: 20 – 30 minutes.

DIRECTIONS: Distribute the "Challenging My Stereotypes" handout to each participant. Tell them:

Working on stereotypes is sometimes an individual activity that requires time and thought. Think about some stereotypes you have that you might want to challenge. For example, are there certain people or groups of people that you won't approach because of various things you've heard about them? Are there certain kinds of food or music you won't try because "only *those* people do that"?

The worksheet is for you to do alone and does not have to be turned in. You can make copies of the handout or get additional handouts if you want to do this activity more than once or share it with a family member or a friend.

Ready? Begin.

After allowing at least 15–20 minutes, give each participant two half sheets of paper and an envelope. Instruct them to write their names on the papers and complete the following statements on both sheets:

1. Something I learned as a result of doing the activity "Challenging My Stereotypes" is . . .

2. Something I am willing to do to challenge stereotypes is . . .

Participants should now have two copies of their completed statements. Ask them to put one copy in the envelope and address it to themselves. The other copy is for them to keep as a reminder of what they wrote. Collect the envelopes. At a later date, give the envelopes back to the participants and have them volunteer to share what they wrote and how well they have lived up to it with the group, along with any difficulties they may have had in challenging stereotypes.

DISCUSSION QUESTIONS:

1. Was it difficult to think and write about your own stereotypes? Why or why not?

2. What are some general obstacles people might encounter when they challenge their stereotypes? How might they overcome these obstacles?

☑ LIST

You will need:

☐ a copy of the "Challenging My Stereotypes" handout for each participant (see page 65)

☐ two half sheets of paper and a small envelope for each participant

3. What are some potential consequences if personal stereotypes are allowed to go unchallenged?

4. Are stereotypes ever a good thing? Please give examples to support your answer.

Challenging My Stereotypes

Stereotypes are oversimplified generalizations about a person or group of people, without regard to the characteristics of the individuals. Stereotypes can be positive or negative, but are generally negative. Stereotypes often resist evidence to the contrary, and pay selective attention to people who fit the stereotype as proof of its "truth." Stereotypes influence how we relate to others and our attitudes about them, and can serve as barriers to genuine relationships. Stereotypes can cause others to feel disrespected and misunderstood.

I have a stereotype about _____.
(Describe the group of people you have the stereotype about. An example could be women, people with red hair, lawyers, politicians, and so on. Remember, we all have stereotypes about different groups of people.)

The following is a description of the stereotype I have about the above group:

The information or evidence I have that supports this stereotype is:

The information or evidence I have that does not support this stereotype is:

How does this stereotype impact what I think, how I feel, how I behave, and how I interact with members of this group?

How do I benefit from keeping this stereotype?

How do I lose by keeping this stereotype?

What can I do to challenge this stereotype?

How should I deal with peers, family members, and friends who help perpetuate this stereotype?

The good things you need to succeed in life are called Developmental Assets™. This activity is designed to help you build those assets, especially Asset 34, Cultural Competence.

CLAIMING OUR NAMES

FOCUS: Participants learn the value of people's names and how mocking a person's name can be hurtful.

☑ LIST

You will need:

☐ a copy of the "Claiming Our Names" handout for each participant (see page 67)

ADDITIONAL ASSETS: Asset 4, Caring Neighborhood; Asset 33, Interpersonal Competence; and Asset 38, Self-Esteem.

TIME REQUIRED: Two 45 – 60 minute meetings over one week.

DIRECTIONS: Ask participants the following questions, recording the number who respond to each question (to be shared again during the group discussion):

1. **Raise your hand if someone has ever made fun of your name.**
2. **Raise your hand if you have ever made fun of someone else's name.**
3. **Raise your hand if you have ever suggested to someone that they shorten their name or get a nickname because you thought the name was too strange or hard to pronounce.**
4. **Raise your hand if someone has ever suggested you shorten your name or adopt a nickname because they thought your name was too strange or hard to pronounce.**

   I want you to conduct interviews that gather information about people's names. Contact people you know who have names or nicknames you think are unusual or unique, or have names that others ridicule. I'd like everyone to talk to at least three people.

Distribute the interview questionnaires. Ask each participant to tally her or his results, which will be added to the group results the next time you meet.

When the participants bring in their survey results at your second meeting, calculate all the responses. Share them with the group and compare them with the participants' own responses to the questions asked during the first half of this activity.

DISCUSSION QUESTIONS:

1. Did anyone have any problems conducting the survey?
2. How do your individual results compare to the group results?
3. Did you learn anything interesting as a result of being involved in this activity?
4. Do you think doing this activity might change your personal behavior? If so, how?

Claiming Our Names

Below are questions meant to gather information on people's names. Interview at least three people you know who have names or nicknames you think are unusual or unique.

	1	2	3
What is your name?			
Can you tell me the national origin of your name?			
Why did you parents give you your name?			
Does your name have a specific meaning?			
If yes, what does your name mean?			
Do people ever mispronounce your name?			
If yes, how do you respond when people mispronounce your name?			
Has anyone ever tried to shorten or change your name?			
Has anyone ever made fun of your name?			
If yes, what did they say?			
What do you like about your name?			

Thank you so much for participating in this survey about names.

The good things you need to succeed in life are called Developmental Assets™. This activity is designed to help you build those assets, especially Asset 34, Cultural Competence.

This handout may be reproduced for educational, noncommercial uses only (with this copyright line): From *Make a World of Difference: 50 Asset-Building Activities to Help Teens Explore Diversity* by Dawn C. Oparah. Copyright © 2006 by Search Institute℠; 800-888-7828; www.search-institute.org. All rights reserved.

FOCUS: Participants complete an inventory of their cultural competence skills.

ADDITIONAL ASSETS: Asset 9, Service to Others; Asset 16, High Expectations; and Asset 22, School Engagement.

TIME REQUIRED: 30 – 45 minutes.

DIRECTIONS: Tell participants:

Your generation will live and work in a diverse world. It is very important for you to have the skill sets necessary to successfully navigate in that world.

Distribute the "Cultural Competence Checklist" handout to each participant. Ask participants to read the list and place a plus (+) sign in front of all the things they feel they have done or mastered. Allow participants at least 10–15 minutes to complete the checklist. By a show of hands, see which participants have the most plus signs on their papers. Ask them to share their experiences in the areas that have plus signs.

Ask participants to check (✓) each area they would like to become more skilled at or master and to circle the three areas they want to make their highest priority.

Divide the larger group into four or five smaller teams. Ask participants to share with their team the areas they selected as their top three priorities. Ask them to discuss with each other what the challenges, barriers, and opportunities might be in trying to implement the priorities.

DISCUSSION QUESTIONS:

1. Which priorities did you choose and why?
2. Were there common themes to your priorities and the priorities chosen by the members of your group?
3. What benefit is it to you as a group and as individuals to become more culturally competent?

Cultural Competence Checklist

■ I am aware of how many different cultures and languages are represented in my school and community.

■ I am aware of my own cultural biases, prejudices, misinformation, and ethnocentrism.

■ I challenge myself on a regular basis to learn more about other cultures.

■ I accept the idea that certain words, tones of voice, or actions might be appropriate for one person while also being offensive to another.

■ I understand that people may identify with more than one culture.

■ I am enrolled in a course or group that promotes cultural competence and/or diversity awareness.

■ In school, I try to help my teachers and peers by providing them with relevant information from a variety of cultures.

■ I believe all cultures should have universal rights.

■ I invite people from other cultures to be featured speakers and/or presenters at organizations in which I'm involved.

■ I invite people from other cultures to visit my home.

■ In school, I challenge myself and others to research information beyond textbooks about other cultures that are relevant to classroom topics.

■ I look for opportunities to appreciate and value difference in class discussions, assignments, and extracurricular activities.

■ I learn by research and inquiry what it is like to "walk a mile in someone else's shoes" before judging a person's customs and practices.

■ I work to eradicate cultural ignorance.

■ I help myself and others become critical thinkers by encouraging them to ask questions and seek answers to their questions.

■ I strive to learn from others about their diverse backgrounds and see them as resources for my own cultural education.

■ I work to call people from diverse backgrounds by their correct names. This includes asking for help with pronunciation, helping my peers learn to say the names correctly, and not offering to change or shorten their names, or give them nicknames just because it's easier for me.

■ I ask people how they identify themselves, rather than assuming a particular nationality or birthplace based on how they look.

■ I try not to assume anything about another person or group based on stereotypes.

■ I identify and challenge stereotypes of various cultures that might arise in movies, literature, textbooks, or TV.

Everyone benefits by becoming more culturally competent!

The good things you need to succeed in life are called Developmental Assets™. This activity is designed to help you build those assets, especially Asset 34, Cultural Competence.

27   THE CIVIL RIGHTS MOVEMENT

FOCUS: Participants explore diversity issues while learning about an important period in U.S. and Canadian history.

☑ LIST

You will need:
- ☐ newsprint and a marker

ADDITIONAL ASSETS: Asset 3, Other Adult Relationships; Asset 4, Caring Neighborhood; and Asset 14, Adult Role Models.

TIME REQUIRED: Two 45– to 60-minute meetings over one week.

DIRECTIONS: Share the following with participants:

Some people think of the phrase "the Civil Rights movement" as meaning only that period between 1950 and 1970. For many groups (including racial minorities, sexual minorities, women, and other groups) that have been deprived of legal rights, important civil rights issues have existed as far back as the beginning of our country and as recently as today. Taking that large time span into account, what civil rights issues can you think of?

Allow participants approximately 15 minutes to brainstorm various civil rights issues and record them on newsprint. If participants have trouble getting started, ask them to think about when various groups were allowed to vote, own property, marry outside of their race or gender, and so on.

Once the group is finished brainstorming, state the following:

Look at the list we've created. I'd like you to choose one of these issues and research it by interviewing an elder in your family, school, neighborhood, or congregation who can either remember the issue personally or remembers hearing stories about the issue you have chosen. Ask the elder to try to recall the general position of her or his family, or if family members had different opinions. Ask what the political climate was at the time. Ask if there are any family journals, diaries, or other documents where family history was recorded.

Next, draw a family tree of the elder's relatives who were alive at the time of the civil rights issue that you have chosen. Write their names and their likely position on the issue and why they might have held that position.

When you have finished your research, write a few paragraphs that describe the elder's family during the time of the civil rights issue. Include in the essay whether you would have agreed with or opposed the opinions, knowing everything you know today. State your reasons for your position.

Depending on available time, allow anywhere from a day to a week for participants to complete this assignment. After the interviews are completed, ask participants to share their papers and family trees with the entire group.

DISCUSSION QUESTIONS:

1. What was the benefit of doing this exercise?

2. What did you learn about the elder that you did not know before?

3. Based on what you learned, what can you say in general about the time period in which the issue arose? How did people in different areas of society react to the issue? What other issues were also important at the time?

4. Looking toward the future, what civil rights issues do you think might arise?

FOCUS: Participants explore some of the stereotypes surrounding mental illness sufferers and brainstorm ways to combat those stereotypes.

ADDITIONAL ASSETS: Asset 4, Caring Neighborhood; Asset 27, Equality and Social Justice; and Asset 38, Self-Esteem.

TIME REQUIRED: 45 – 60 minutes.

DIRECTIONS: Before the activity begins, write the following definitions on a whiteboard or posted piece of newsprint:

- Bipolar disorder, or manic depression, is a brain disorder. A person with bipolar disorder will go through episodes of mania (highs) and depression (lows). Symptoms of mania include racing speech and thoughts, increased energy, and poor judgment. Symptoms of depression include a depressed mood, appetite loss, and thoughts of suicide.

- Schizophrenia is a brain disorder that affects a person's ability to think clearly, distinguish reality from fantasy, and relate to others. Symptoms can include hallucinations, hearing voices, and paranoia.

- Obsessive-compulsive disorder (OCD) is an anxiety disorder in which people have recurring thoughts, fears, or worries (obsessions) that they try to ease through rituals (compulsions). Symptoms can include constant checking, excessive fear of germs, and a need for exactness and order.

- Anorexia nervosa is an eating disorder in which people intentionally starve themselves, either by undereating, vomiting, excessive exercise, laxative and diuretic abuse, or a combination of these. Symptoms often include an intense fear of gaining weight, food rituals (such as not eating in public), and depression.

- Attention Deficit Hyperactivity disorder (ADHD) is a brain disorder in which people can have difficulty concentrating, sitting still, and keeping impulses in check. Symptoms can also include fidgeting, excessive talking, and forgetfulness.

When participants arrive, divide them into five teams. Assign each team a posted mental illness category, a large sheet of newsprint, and markers. Give participants the following instructions:

I want you to brainstorm for a few minutes about what a typical person with your assigned mental illness might look like. When you're finished, make a life-size outline of a person on your sheet of newsprint. (Make sure to leave enough space around the outline for writing.) Then, write down some words and phrases that describe this "typical person" around the edges of your outline. For example, is the person a

☑ LIST

You will need:

- ☐ a copy of the "Mental Illness Fact Sheet" for each participant (see page 74)

- ☐ newsprint (large enough to make an outline of a life-size person; if large newsprint isn't available, you can also tape several sheets together)

- ☐ markers

- ☐ whiteboard or newsprint and a marker

man or a woman? What sort of job does he or she have? What are her or his hobbies? Also include any stereotypical words or phrases that might be associated with the mental illness.

Allow participants at least 20 minutes to complete their outlines. When they are finished, have each team share some of the words and phrases they've chosen and explain why they picked them. Once every team has shared its outline, give each participant a copy of the "Mental Illness Fact Sheet" handout. Read the handout aloud or allow participants to take turns reading aloud. Participants should write down key phrases from the information about their team's assigned mental illness on the inside of their outlines. Once they are finished, go over the following discussion questions.

DISCUSSION QUESTIONS:

1. Looking at what we've written around our outlines and the information we've just learned from our fact sheet, is it really possible to say what a "typical" person living with a mental illness looks like? Why or why not?

2. Do you think people with mental illnesses are treated differently than people with physical illnesses? If so, what are the differences in treatment? Why do you think those differences exist?

3. What are some ways that communities might help combat the stereotypes attached to mental illness?

4. What are some ways that you, as an individual, might help combat the stereotypes attached to mental illness?

Mental Illness Fact Sheet

Bipolar disorder

- Men and women are equally likely to develop bipolar disorder.[1]
- The average age of onset for a first manic episode is the early 20s.[1]
- The illness tends to be genetic, but there are clearly environmental factors that influence whether the illness will occur in a particular person. Bipolar disorder can skip generations and take different forms in different individuals.[2]

Schizophrenia

- Schizophrenia occurs in 1% of the world's population.[3]
- Schizophrenia may affect people of all races and social classes. It is usually first diagnosed in people in their teens and 20s.[3]
- News and entertainment media tend to link mental illnesses, including schizophrenia, to criminal violence. Most people with schizophrenia, however, are not violent toward others but are withdrawn and prefer to be left alone.[4]

Obsessive-Compulsive disorder (OCD)

- Approximately 3.3 million American adults ages 18 to 54, or about 2.3% of people in this age group in a given year, have OCD.[1]
- The first symptoms of OCD often surface during childhood or adolescence.[1]
- OCD is not caused by family problems or attitudes learned in childhood, such as an emphasis on cleanliness, or a belief that certain thoughts are dangerous or unacceptable.[5]

Anorexia nervosa

- Anorexia primarily affects people in their teens and 20s, but studies report the disorder in children as young as six and individuals as old as 76.[6]
- Certain personality traits common in persons with anorexia nervosa are low self-esteem, social isolation (which usually occurs after the behavior associated with anorexia nervosa begins), and perfectionism. These people tend to be good students and excellent athletes.[7]
- Eating disorders tend to run in families, with female relatives most often affected. A girl has a 10- to 20-times higher risk of developing anorexia nervosa, for instance, if she has a sibling with the disease. This finding suggests that genetic factors may predispose some people to eating disorders.[7]

Attention Deficit Hyperactivity disorder (ADHD)

- ADHD, one of the most common mental disorders in children and adolescents, affects an estimated 4.1% of young people ages 9 to 17 in a six-month period.[1]
- About two to three times more boys than girls are affected.[1]
- ADHD usually becomes evident in preschool or early elementary years. The disorder frequently persists into adolescence and occasionally into adulthood.[1]

[1] "The Numbers Count: Mental Disorders in America," National Institute of Mental Health, 2001.

[2] "About Pediatric Bipolar Disorder," Child and Adolescent Bipolar Foundation, 2005.

[3] The World Fellowship for Schizophrenia and Allied Disorders (www.world-schizophrenia.org), 2005.

[4] "When Someone Has Schizophrenia," National Institute of Mental Health, 2001.

[5] "Step on a Crack ... Obsessive-Compulsive Disorder," National Institute of Mental Health, 2001.

[6] Anorexia Nervosa and Related Eating Disorders, Inc. (www.anred.com), 2005.

[7] "Anorexia Nervosa," National Alliance on Mental Illness (www.nami.org), 2005.

The good things you need to succeed in life are called Developmental Assets™. This activity is designed to help you build those assets, especially Asset 34, Cultural Competence.

29 — **REMEMBERING BIAS**

FOCUS: Participants remember a time when they felt they were victims of bias as a way to discuss the negative effects of bias in our culture.

ADDITIONAL ASSETS: Asset 4, Caring Neighborhood; Asset 5, Caring School Climate; and Asset 7, Community Values Youth.

TIME REQUIRED: 45 – 60 minutes.

DIRECTIONS: While distributing the "Remembering Bias" handout, tell participants:

> **All of us, at some point in our lives, have felt that people were making negative judgments about us or treating us unfairly based on a personal characteristic that we may or may not have any control over. This kind of treatment is often the result of bias, an unfair preference for or dislike of something.**
>
> **Do you remember a time when you felt you were a victim of bias? A time when you felt you were treated differently because of some characteristic, such as the way you dress, your personal style, your speech, your skin color, your gender, your grades, or your age? I want you to recall that time and record what happened as legibly as possible. Do not write your name on your paper.**

Allow participants 10 to 12 minutes to write their answers. Once participants are finished, collect all the papers. Shuffle them and randomly redistribute them. Tell participants not to tell anyone if they happen to receive their own paper.

Ask participants to take turns reading aloud the personal stories on the paper in front of them.

DISCUSSION QUESTIONS:
1. How did listening to all the stories make you feel?
2. Were you surprised at how some of your fellow group members handled their situations?
3. Were there any general themes that emerged in terms of the types of bias and the responses to it?
4. How did the people who experienced bias feel?
5. Can you remember a time when you might have been biased against another person?
6. How do assumptions get in the way of how we treat other people?
7. What can we do to minimize the assumptions we might have about another person?
8. How can we challenge our personal biases, stereotypes, and assumptions?

☑ LIST

You will need:

☐ a copy of the "Remembering Bias" handout for each participant (see page 76)

☐ pencils or pens

Remembering Bias

DIRECTIONS: Think of a time when you felt someone was biased against you because of your gender, race, appearance, age, manner of speaking, etc. Write about that experience in the spaces provided below.

What happened? How did you know you were being unfairly judged?	**How did you feel?** What were your thoughts and feelings when this situation occurred?
What did you say or do?	**Would you say or do anything differently if the biased behavior happened again?**

30 — TIME OF YOUR LIFE

FOCUS: Participants explore ageism and its effects on young people and elders.

ADDITIONAL ASSETS: Asset 3, Other Adult Relationships; Asset 8, Youth as Resources; and Asset 14, Adult Role Models.

TIME REQUIRED: 45 – 60 minutes.

DIRECTIONS: Before the activity, post your signs around the room. When participants arrive, share the following with them:

We all have opinions about what activities are appropriate at various ages. Oftentimes, however, our opinions aren't based on fact but on what we've seen and heard, either in real life or in the media. When people make judgments about others based solely on their age, it's called *ageism*. An example of ageism would be when a company decides not to hire anyone over 50 because they are "too old." Another would be saying that teenagers can't be trusted with important tasks because they're "too young."

Point out the signs around the room and say:

These are age ranges. I'm going to read a list of activities that many people do. I want you to go and stand by the sign that shows how old you think people are who typically do that activity. If you can't decide, stand by "Don't Know."

After you read each one, pause and have participants share reasons why they think people have to be a certain age to take part in the activity. Use this list of activities, changing items as necessary to better fit your group:

- Ride a bike
- Get a piercing
- Become pregnant
- Drive alone
- Have a summer job or internship
- Watch R-rated movies
- Buy a sports car
- Stay out until midnight
- Drink alcohol
- Work as a waiter or waitress
- Wear a short skirt and high heels
- Live alone

LIST

You will need:

- ☐ markers
- ☐ newsprint
- ☐ tape
- ☐ eight large signs posted in the room labeled UNDER 10, 10–20, 21–30, 31–40, 41–50, 51–60, OVER 60, DON'T KNOW

- Have others make decisions for them
- Play basketball
- Enroll in college
- Wear a hearing aid
- Dance
- Have friends in their 20s
- Get married
- Receive a kidney transplant
- Knit, crochet, or sew
- Go on a date

DISCUSSION QUESTIONS:

1. Have you ever experienced or witnessed prejudice or discrimination based on age? Please explain.

2. Thinking about the list of activities we went through, why do you think some of them seem tied to a certain age range?

3. As a young person, can you draw similarities between how you are treated and how elderly people are treated? If so, what are they? Are there any differences in how these two groups are treated? If so, what are they?

4. Are there certain activities that people can definitely be "too old" to do? If so, what are they and what makes you think that?

5. What are the benefits to knowing people of different ages?

6. What effects can ageism have on older people? on young people?

31

THE HORROR OF HATE

FOCUS: Participants reflect on and discuss the negative results of homophobia.

☑ LIST

You will need:

☐ a copy of "The Matthew Shepard Tragedy" handout for each participant (see page 80)

☐ discarded magazines and newspapers

☐ scissors

☐ glue

☐ construction paper

☐ colored pencils or markers

ADDITIONAL ASSETS: Asset 7, Community Values Youth; Asset 10, Safety; and Asset 36, Peaceful Conflict Resolution.

TIME REQUIRED: 45 – 60 minutes.

DIRECTIONS: Distribute a copy of "The Matthew Shepard Tragedy" handout, paper, and a pencil or marker to each participant. Tell them:

I want you to read this true story. When you are finished, use the supplies to make a collage expressing your thoughts and feelings in response to the story.

Ask volunteers to share their thoughts.

DISCUSSION QUESTIONS:

1. Why was Matthew Shepard killed?

2. What is present in our society that allows violence toward GLBT people to be tolerated?

3. Should Matthew have hidden his sexual orientation for his own safety?

4. What did Matthew do wrong?

5. What does it mean to "blame the victim"?

6. Does society have a responsibility to protect people like Matthew? Why or why not?

7. What message does our community send out about GLBT people?

8. Do you think hate crime laws are necessary? Why or why not?

9. What can we learn from this situation?

The Matthew Shepard Tragedy

Matthew Shepard was a 21-year-old college student who was brutally tortured and murdered in a hate crime. Shepard, a student at the University of Wyoming, was robbed and attacked by two men near Laramie, Wyoming, on the night of October 6, 1998, because of his homosexuality. Shepard died from his wounds several days later. His killers are both currently serving life sentences in prison.

Background

Shepard was born in Casper, the eldest son of Dennis Shepard and Judy Peck Shepard. He attended Crest Hill Grade School, Dean Morgan Junior High, and the first two years of high school at Natrona County High School, and was a member of St. Mark's Episcopal Church. Shepard spent his junior and senior years of high school at The American School In Switzerland, graduating in 1995. Shepard later attended Catawba College and Casper College before moving to Denver. He then became a first-year political science major at the University of Wyoming.

The attack

Shepard met Aaron James McKinney and Russell Arthur Henderson in a bar. After he confided to them that he was gay, they deceived him into leaving with them in their car. He was robbed, severely beaten, tied to a fence, and left to die. McKinney and Henderson also found out his address, intending to burgle his home. Shepard was discovered 18 hours later, alive and unconscious.

Shepard suffered a fracture from the back of his head to the front of his right ear. He also had catastrophic brain stem damage, which affected his body's ability to regulate heartbeat, body temperature, and other vital signs. There were also about a dozen small lacerations around his head, face, and neck. His injuries were deemed too severe for doctors to operate. Shepard never regained consciousness and remained on full life support. He died at 12:53 a.m. on October 12 at Poudre Valley Hospital in Fort Collins, Colorado.

The blood on Shepard's face had been partly washed away by tears, indicating that he had been conscious for some time after the beating. He had been pistol-whipped 18 times with a .357-caliber revolver.

Police arrested McKinney and Henderson shortly thereafter, finding the bloody gun as well as the victim's shoes and credit card in their truck. The two murderers had attempted to get alibis from their girlfriends.

The trial

It is believed that McKinney and Henderson had posed as homosexuals in order to trick Shepard into trusting them. During court cases both of the defendants used varying stories to defend their actions. Most notably they used the "gay panic defense," arguing that they were driven to temporary insanity by Shepard's alleged homosexual advances toward them. At another point they stated that they had only wanted to rob Shepard, and never intended to kill him.

Henderson pleaded guilty on April 5, 1999, and agreed to testify against McKinney to avoid the death penalty; he received two consecutive life sentences, without the possibility of parole. The jury in McKinney's trial found him guilty of first-degree murder. As it began to deliberate on the death penalty, Shepard's parents brokered a deal, resulting in McKinney also receiving two consecutive life terms without the possibility of parole. Shepard's parents stated, "We are giving him life in the memory of one who no longer lives."

The good things you need to succeed in life are called Developmental Assets™. This activity is designed to help you build those assets, especially Asset 34, Cultural Competence.

32 THAT'S SEXIST!

FOCUS: Participants identify how sexism is used in language, behavior, attitudes, policies, and institutional beliefs, and discuss how to challenge sexism in all areas of their lives.

☑ LIST

You will need:

☐ whiteboard; newsprint and a marker

ADDITIONAL ASSETS: Asset 8, Youth as Resources; Asset 16, High Expectations; and Asset 38, Self-Esteem.

TIME REQUIRED: 30 – 50 minutes.

DIRECTIONS: Write the following definitions of sexism from *Merriam-Webster's Collegiate Dictionary* (11th ed.) on a whiteboard or newsprint so that everyone can read it:

> **sexism: 1** *: prejudice or discrimination based on sex; esp. : discrimination against women* **2** *: behavior, conditions, or attitudes that foster stereotypes of social roles based on sex*

On separate sheets of newsprint, list the following possible types of sexism: beliefs, behaviors, language, and policies. Ask participants the following questions, recording their responses on the appropriate piece of newsprint:

Describe a situation in which sexism occurred. Your responses can come from real-life situations: print media (including magazines, newspapers, books, and brochures); electronic media (including TV, movies, and radio); athletic programs; schools; faith organizations; government institutions; law enforcement; corporations; and other organizations.

- **Describe an instance when someone's beliefs were expressed in a sexist way.** (List the responses on the newsprint titled "Beliefs.")
- **Describe an instance when the behaviors of others were expressed in a sexist way.** (List the responses on the newsprint titled "Behaviors.")
- **Describe a time when the language used by others was sexist.** (List the responses on the newsprint titled "Language.")
- **Describe a time when policies advanced sexism simply by the nature of the policy.** (List the responses on the newsprint titled "Policies.")

DISCUSSION QUESTIONS:

1. How can you challenge sexist beliefs, behaviors, language, and policies in a healthy way? Describe a sexist situation, and as a group we'll try to come up with a response that challenges the stereotype without being confrontational. (Repeat this exercise three or four times.)

2. Does sexism have harmful effects on our society? If so, what are they?

## 33

ON BEING ETHNOCENTRIC

FOCUS: Participants explore how their upbringing affects how they perceive and look at people who don't belong to their cultural or ethnic group.

☑ LIST

You will need:

☐ a copy of the "Cultural Ethnocentrism" handout for each participant (see page 83)

☐ three large signs posted in the room labeled AGREE, DISAGREE, and NOT SURE

ADDITIONAL ASSETS: Asset 1, Family Support; Asset 2, Positive Family Communication; and Asset 20, Time at Home.

TIME REQUIRED: 20 – 30 minutes.

DIRECTIONS: Ask participants how they would define the word "ethnocentric." After listening to their responses, distribute the "Cultural Ethnocentrism" handout and ask them what they think of the definition on the paper; have them support their responses with examples.

Review the definitions for "acculturation" and "enculturation" and instruct participants to think of a time when they felt they were being acculturated as a child. Ask them to share some examples.

Tell participants:

I'm going to read some of the statements from the "Statements on Culture" section of the handout. When I read a statement, go stand by the posted sign that most closely represents your answer.

Read one statement. Once participants have had a chance to decide their answers and stand by the corresponding sign, ask each group's members to explain why they chose their position and to support their answer with examples. Repeat these steps for as many statements as you'd like.

DISCUSSION QUESTIONS:

1. What are some benefits to learning about other cultures?

2. Without devaluing our own culture, how can we learn to appreciate, value, and celebrate other cultures?

3. What can we do when people make culturally insensitive remarks?

4. Suggest some things we can do in our school and in our community to appreciate cultures different from our own.

Cultural Ethnocentrism

Ethnocentrism is the tendency of people to put their own group at the center of their worldview; to see things only through the lens of their own culture; and to use the standards of their culture to judge others. An ethnocentric point of view usually leads to a biased belief in the inferiority of other groups and, at the extreme, to cultural bigotry. The negative effects of ethnocentrism can lead to prejudice, the use of power and privilege to discriminate against another group, and sometimes violence.

Acculturation is the process of conditioning a child to the patterns or customs of a culture; the process of adapting to a new or different culture; or the mutual influence of different cultures in close contact.

Enculturation is the method used to cause one to adapt to the prevailing patterns of one's society; the process of being socialized into one's culture.

Statements on Culture (for discussion):

1. Everyone is ethnocentric.

2. Each culture thinks its own ways are superior.

3. We see life through the lenses of our own cultural beliefs and values.

4. Our cultural beliefs and values influence how we behave and respond to events.

5. Our culture and values influence what we see, hear, and feel and how we see, hear, and feel.

6. What seems sensible, rational, logical, and important to a person in one culture may seem silly, irrational, ridiculous, and unimportant to someone from outside that culture.

7. When people talk about other cultures, they tend to describe differences and not similarities.

8. It requires patience, experience, and a willingness to learn in order to understand the many nuances of another culture.

9. Understanding another culture is an ongoing process and not something we can complete once and for all.

10. Not every conflict involving people who are different is caused by a cultural problem.

11. Cultural conflict does not disappear because we decide to ignore it.

12. Every culture establishes norms concerning how to respond to expressions of respect and disrespect in the culture.

13. Improving intercultural relationships and valuing diversity require an open mind, humility, patience, flexibility, tolerance for ambiguity, and a sense of humor.

## 34

CHANGING YOUR RACE

FOCUS: Participants visualize being a member of a different race to understand the impact race has on our lives.

ADDITIONAL ASSETS: Asset 4, Caring Neighborhood; Asset 5, Caring School Climate; and Asset 7, Community Values Youth.

TIME REQUIRED: 30 – 45 minutes.

DIRECTIONS: Tell participants the following:

> **The history of race in North America is complicated, especially because of laws concerning race and segregation that persisted long after emancipation. To illustrate the role that race plays in our lives, I'm going to lead you through a visualization exercise that allows you to imagine being part of another race.**
>
> **Get comfortable and close your eyes. Choose a race you will become that is different from the race you were born into.**

Slowly read the following, pausing to allow participants to imagine their responses:

> **Imagine that tomorrow when you wake up, you are no longer the same race you went to sleep as. You are now a member of a different race. Your family also changed races with you.** (pause) **Imagine you are waiting at a school bus stop. What do your peers say to you, if anything?** (pause) **Go to your first class and talk to the friends you normally chat with. What is their response? Do they have any other friends of your race?** (pause) **In your second class, how do your fellow students respond?** (pause) **How about your teachers? What have they said so far, if anything? Do they treat you the same, or differently?** (pause) **Continue through your morning classes. What happens?** (pause) **Imagine yourself eating lunch. What do your friends say and do?** (pause) **Complete the school day, class by class. What happens?** (pause) **If you participate in any extracurricular activities, go to those activities. What happens?** (pause) **If you belong to a faith organization, imagine you and your family attending as a different race. Are there any reactions from the members of your faith organization?** (pause) **Go for a walk in your neighborhood; say hi to your neighbors as you pass them. What is their response? Are any of them the same race as you?** (pause) **Imagine the day is over and you are back to being a member of your birth race. Review the day and all your experiences. How did the day go?** (pause) **What are your thoughts and feelings about the whole day?** (pause) **Please write down some things that stick in your mind about this day.**

DISCUSSION QUESTIONS:

1. How easy or difficult was it to participate in this exercise?

2. What were some of the thoughts that came up for you as we went through this exercise?

3. Were you frustrated at any point during the exercise?

4. How was your life the same as a member of a different race? How was it different?

5. Is race still an issue in our society? Why or why not?

6. What are some things you thought or learned as a result of doing this activity?

7. What are the larger lessons and implications for us as a society in doing this exercise?

EDUCATIONAL EXTENSION:

As a group, read and discuss *Black Like Me,* by John Howard Griffin. In the late 1950s, Griffin, a white journalist concerned about race relations, used medication and dyes to darken his skin. This memoir chronicles his experiences traveling as a black man through the American South.

35 CLASS ACTS

FOCUS: Participants offer positive suggestions for navigating class differences.

You will need:

☐ four index cards or sheets of paper

☐ pencils or pens

ADDITIONAL ASSETS: Asset 15, Positive Peer Influence; Asset 33, Interpersonal Competence; and Asset 36, Peaceful Conflict Resolution.

TIME REQUIRED: 45 – 60 minutes.

DIRECTIONS: Before the participants arrive, write each of these skit starters on an index card or sheet of paper:

- Your class is going on an overnight field trip next week. The cost is $100 for each person. Everyone has already turned in their checks and permissions slips except one of your friends. He tells you his family can't afford to pay for the trip and he hasn't told anyone but you. What do you do now?

- You're on the basketball team at your local recreation center. After every game the whole team goes to a different player's house for pizza. Your turn is coming up in two days, but you're embarrassed because you live in a very small apartment with your dad, while all the other players and their families live in houses that seem like mansions to you. What do you do now?

- Your family doesn't have a lot of money. You don't get to buy the brand-name clothes your friends wear, but you've gotten good at finding look-alikes at thrift stores. You've never told anyone about this, not even your close friends. One day, a couple of your friends are joking about a girl in your neighborhood, saying, "Look at her shirt. She looks like she lives in a homeless shelter!" What do you do now?

- Your parents tell you they're going to buy you a new car as an early birthday present once you pass your driver's license test. You're so excited you immediately call your best friend to tell him the news. He tells you his parents can't afford to help him buy a car, and told him that he'll have to work after school and over the summer to get one. What do you do now?

Divide the participants into four teams and give each team a skit starter. Challenge them to plan a skit that shows a course of action that would be a positive experience for everyone involved in the situation. Allow 10 minutes for teams to work, then ask each team to present its skit.

DISCUSSION QUESTIONS:

1. Was it challenging to think of solutions that are positive for everyone involved? Why or why not?

2. What gets in the way of positive relationships across class boundaries?

3. What are three things people can do to create and maintain positive relationships with people of all classes?

4. What are some benefits of being friends with people from different classes?

36 BEHIND THE LABELS

FOCUS: Participants learn what it's like to be labeled and treated according to that label.

ADDITIONAL ASSETS: Asset 4, Caring Neighborhood; Asset 37, Personal Power; and Asset 38, Self-Esteem.

TIME REQUIRED: 35 – 55 minutes.

DIRECTIONS: On each index card, write a "label." Possible ideas include jock, cheerleader, millionaire, school dropout, lesbian, smoker, professor, drug addict, prostitute, construction worker, juvenile delinquent, genius, homeless person, farmer. Stick a label on the backs of about one-third of the participants. (Participants should not know the label they have been given.) *Be careful not to give a label to someone who may have characteristics of the stereotypes that go with that particular label.* Choose two or three participants to sit back and be observers. The rest of the group will mill around in the crowd.

Instruct the participants:

Pretend you are at a party. Interact and socialize as you normally would in that type of setting. Everyone, except for the observers, should treat people according to the labels they are wearing without revealing what the label is.

Start the music to begin the simulation. Circulate around the group with the selected observers. Take note of the comments participants are making and how they treat each other.

Stop the exercise when it appears that the participants wearing labels are clued into which label they have been given.

Ask the participants to try to guess what label they are wearing. If they guess correctly, ask them what clues they were given. This exercise can be repeated with different participants wearing new labels.

Ask the observers to share some of their observations of the simulated activities.

DISCUSSION QUESTIONS:

1. How did it feel to be labeled and treated according to that label?
2. Did anyone wearing a label feel ignored or invisible? If yes, what was that like?
3. What assumptions were made about the people wearing labels?
4. What do you think this activity illustrates?
5. How is labeling damaging to others?
6. Are there things you can take from this exercise that will help you in your interactions with others? If so, what are they?

LIST

You will need:

- ☐ CD player and music
- ☐ index cards (one for each participant)
- ☐ tape

THE EFFECTS OF "MALE BASHING"

FOCUS: Participants examine the negative impact of derogatory remarks made toward males.

You will need:

☐ newsprint

☐ markers

ADDITIONAL ASSETS: Asset 7, Community Values Youth; Asset 16, High Expectations; and Asset 38, Self-Esteem.

TIME REQUIRED: 30 – 45 minutes.

DIRECTIONS: Ask the participants:

Do you think society pressures boys and men to conform to a certain way of behaving that is accepted by their peers and others? Explain your answers.

Divide the group into four or five smaller teams. In their teams, ask the participants to write down on newsprint the types of messages that males are given from birth to adulthood. Ask the participants to also write down the "dos and don'ts" of male behavior as prescribed by societal norms. Then, ask each team to write down derogatory terms used to describe males. Remind the participants that boys and men in different cultural groups (ethnic, religious, socioeconomic, and so on) can experience different kinds of pressures, so their responses should be as specific as possible. Once the participants are finished, have them discuss what impact they think these messages, rules, and negative terms have on a young man's behavior. Bring the small teams back into the larger group and have them share what was discussed.

DISCUSSION QUESTIONS:

1. Why are these negative terms that people use to describe men disrespectful, insulting, and hurtful?

2. If a young man does not meet the standard of masculinity prescribed by his society, he may be compared unfavorably to girls, which is considered highly insulting. What might the results of this kind of teasing be?

3. What makes it okay in our society for males to taunt other males?

4. How do you think such treatment impacts male behavior and self-esteem?

5. Why should we eliminate derogatory language about men from our vocabulary?

6. What can we do, either individually or collectively, to minimize male bashing by either gender?

38   ROLE MODELS

FOCUS: Participants study the religious involvement of their role models.

ADDITIONAL ASSETS: Asset 3, Other Adult Relationships; Asset 14, Adult Role Models; and Asset 19, Religious Community.

TIME REQUIRED: 30 – 45 minutes.

DIRECTIONS: Have participants identify some of their well-known role models. For example, participants can name current or former presidents, music stars, actors/actresses, sports stars or social activists. Write these names on a posted piece of newsprint or a whiteboard.

Divide participants into teams of three. Have each team discuss one role model and that person's involvement in religion. (Participants may need to do some research to learn more about the role model.) Have participants discuss the questions below in their teams, then ask for volunteers to share highlights of their discussions with the larger group.

DISCUSSION QUESTIONS:

1. Of the role models we've named who have made significant contributions to society, how involved are they in religion? What impact does that involvement seem to have on them?

2. Does learning about role models' religious involvement change your view of them? Why or why not?

3. Is it important to know about a person's religious involvement before deciding whether to look up to her or him? Why or why not?

☑ LIST

You will need:

☐ whiteboard or newsprint and a marker

☐ a marker

☐ reference materials or Internet access (optional)

Section 3: Practice Activities

39 — FACES

FOCUS: Youth construct puzzles to encourage cultural sensitivity in younger children.

You will need:

- ☐ several pieces of poster board
- ☐ markers
- ☐ discarded family and children's magazines
- ☐ glue sticks
- ☐ sharp scissors
- ☐ zipper-closure food storage bags

ADDITIONAL ASSETS: Asset 8, Youth as Resources; Asset 9, Service to Others; and Asset 18, Youth Programs.

TIME REQUIRED: 45 – 60 minutes. *Note: This activity may take more than one session.*

DIRECTIONS: Before the activity, locate a group or class of kindergarten or first-grade children who can meet with your participants for about 15 minutes during this activity. Form teams of three and give each team a piece of poster board. Give these instructions:

Find pictures that show the faces of children and families from many different backgrounds. Arrange these on the poster board and glue them in place. Use the markers to add words that will help young children understand the importance of getting along with people from different backgrounds. After the glue dries, cut the poster board into 20–25 pieces and put the pieces in a bag.

Once participants are finished making their puzzles, have each team of three work with a small group of children to assemble the puzzles. Encourage participants to ask children questions about the pictures in the puzzle, and to talk with them about the value of similarities and differences among people.

Let the younger children keep the puzzles for future play. Go over the following discussion questions with participants.

DISCUSSION QUESTIONS:

1. What did you learn from the children as you put the puzzle together?
2. Did you hear anything from a child that concerned you? If so, how did you respond to the child who made the comment?
3. What do you think families can do to help their children learn to accept people who are from different backgrounds? What can schools or congregations do?

40 EASY ACCESS

FOCUS: Participants create plans to make their school and/or community accessible to people with a variety of physical disabilities.

ADDITIONAL ASSETS: Asset 8, Youth as Resources; Asset 9, Service to Others; and Asset 10, Safety.

TIME REQUIRED: 45 – 60 minutes.

DIRECTIONS: Have participants work together to create a large map of the building where you are meeting. Be especially careful to include any exits and entrances, stairs, elevators, escalators, and bathrooms. Once they are finished, post the map where everyone can see it.

Next, divide the participants into groups of three. Tell each team the following:

Now that we've made a map of the building, I want each team to take a 10-minute walk around the building with your paper and clipboards. I want you to record anything that might pose a problem to someone with a physical disability. For example, imagine that you came to a flight of stairs. Ask yourself, "How would a person in a wheelchair get around this obstacle? Is there another way to go up or down to a different floor? Are there signs that clearly explain how to do that?" As you walk around, keep other physical factors like crutches, blindness, or deafness in mind, too. (Someone in each team should be in charge of keeping track of time.) Encourage participants to head in different directions to get different perspectives.

When the teams return, have them report on any accessibility issues they noted. Give the participants pushpins and markers to label these spots on the map. After each team's report, ask the larger group to vote on which of the trouble spots is the most significant and which is the most easily fixed. Record these on a separate piece of newsprint. Once the teams have finished sharing their findings, discuss the questions below.

DISCUSSION QUESTIONS:

1. Which of the accessibility trouble spots could our group work to fix?
2. Which of the accessibility trouble spots will need key leaders and/or organizations working together to fix them?
3. Which accessibility trouble spots will need the work of a professional (such as an electrician or a carpenter)?
4. How did it make you feel to examine the building through the eyes of a person with a physical disability?

☑ LIST

You will need:

- ☐ two large sheets of newsprint
- ☐ tape
- ☐ markers
- ☐ clipboards
- ☐ pencils or pens
- ☐ writing paper
- ☐ pushpins

5. Should all buildings be accessible to people with physical disabilities? Why or why not?

EDUCATIONAL EXTENSION: If your group meets at a school, decide which accessibility trouble spots your group will fix and which the group wants to refer to a school administrator. Work together to create a list of tasks and a plan for the work and the referrals to take place. Set up a time frame for when these actions will take place. Consider presenting the proposed changes at a school assembly, school committee or board meeting, or parent–teacher association meeting. Follow up in a later session to learn what responses were received in order to complete accessibility improvements and find out what referrals were made for professional consultations.

41

THE GRAND MIXER

FOCUS: Participants get to know each other in greater depth as a prelude to future personal interactions beyond the current group.

FOCUS: Participants get to know each other in greater depth as a prelude to future personal interactions beyond the current group.

☑ LIST

You will need:

☐ a copy of "The Grand Mixer" handout for each participant (see page 94)

☐ pencils or pens

ADDITIONAL ASSETS: Asset 15, Positive Peer Influence; Asset 33, Interpersonal Competence; and Asset 39, Sense of Purpose.

TIME REQUIRED: 30 – 45 minutes.

DIRECTIONS: Tell participants the following:

The more frequently people communicate with each other, the wider their boundaries and friendships become. Today's activity will give everyone an opportunity to get to know members of this group better.

Distribute "The Grand Mixer" handout. Tell participants:

You will have several minutes to talk with and listen to a variety of people from the group. The Grand Mixer questions are a way to help the conversation flow. You can ask any questions on the list. When you are paired up with someone, you will both ask questions and listen to each other's responses. Ground rules for this activity are listed on the handout.

Review the ground rules with participants and solicit questions for clarification. Ask the group if there are any additional rules that should be added to the list. If so, have participants write them on their handouts.

Ask the participants to pair up with someone they don't know well. Give the pairs five to seven minutes to talk with each other and then stop them. Ask them to switch and pair up with someone else they don't know very well. This can go on for three to four rounds. After the final round, bring the group back together to discuss the activity.

DISCUSSION QUESTIONS:

1. How easy or difficult was it to do this activity? Explain.

2. How many of you wanted to continue conversations after time was up?

3. What was something interesting you learned about another participant you didn't know before?

4. Did anything in your conversations surprise you?

5. What things did you find you had in common with others?

6. What are some things you admired or respected about another person?

7. In doing this activity, did you learn anything about yourself?

8. How do we extend what we have learned about getting to know others beyond this activity?

The Grand Mixer

General Ground Rules

- Treat each of your conversation partners with respect.

- Listen carefully to what your partner has to say.

- One person talks at a time.

- If you are talking about others not in the group today, don't use their real names.

- It's okay to have differing opinions. Don't feel you must agree.

- If you feel offended, say so and why you feel that way.

- Unless the whole group agrees otherwise, what is said in the room stays in the room.

- Use the space below to add any rules the group creates:

Questions

You can ask any of the questions below of your partner. They don't have to be in any particular order.

1. What kind of music do you like to listen to?

2. What do you like to do for fun?

3. What is one of the greatest lessons you have learned in life so far?

4. What advice would you give to your own children about life and growing up?

5. Who are the people you admire most in the world and why?

6. What are some of your goals for the future?

7. What is your greatest fear?

8. If you had 3 wishes, what would you wish for?

9. If you could go anywhere in the world, where would you go and why?

10. If you could give our country's leaders some advice, what would you tell them?

11. What do you think is the hardest thing about growing up?

12. If you could change one thing about your school, what would it be?

13. What is one thing you wish more people knew about you?

42   ENTERING YOUR DISCOMFORT ZONE

FOCUS: Participants place themselves in unfamiliar and uncomfortable settings as a way of understanding others and themselves.

ADDITIONAL ASSETS: Asset 4, Caring Neighborhood; Asset 7, Community Values Youth; and Asset 33, Interpersonal Competence.

TIME REQUIRED: Two 45- to 60-minute meetings over one week.

DIRECTIONS: Give participants the following instructions:

☑ **LIST**

You will need:

☐ notepads or small journals (one for each participant)

> Staying in one's social group can feel very easy and safe. However, some of the greatest learning comes from going beyond our comfort zones. Many of the great people of the world became great because of their willingness to explore the unknown and go beyond their internal and external boundaries.
>
> I want you to spend the next week purposely putting yourself in situations and settings that go beyond your normal comfort zone. In order for the activity to be personally meaningful to you, you have to choose environments that are unfamiliar and slightly uncomfortable. Some suggestions might include:
> - A different seat on the school bus
> - A senior citizens center or nursing home
> - A playground in another neighborhood
> - A different faith worship service
> - A restaurant where the cuisine is foreign to you
> - A part of town where another language is spoken
>
> Keep a journal of what happens. Describe the settings you chose. Describe how others reacted to you, your thoughts, how you felt, and what you learned about yourself. After the activity, prepare a talk about your experiences that you can share with the group.

Note: Participants' safety should always be the facilitator's first priority. Participants should have the consent and support of their parents or caregivers before participating in this activity, as well as supervision if traveling to unfamiliar neighborhoods.

DISCUSSION QUESTIONS:

1. How easy or difficult was it for you to do this activity?

2. What did you learn from doing this activity?

3. Of what value was this activity to you? How can it help you in the future?

COVER STORIES

FOCUS: Participants learn how making judgments based on appearances can often lead to incorrect conclusions.

☑ LIST

You will need:

- ☐ photocopies or print-outs of eight book covers (make color copies if possible)
- ☐ tape or correction fluid
- ☐ whiteboard or newsprint and a marker

ADDITIONAL ASSETS: Asset 22, School Engagement; Asset 25, Reading for Pleasure; and Asset 32, Planning and Decision Making.

TIME REQUIRED: 30 – 45 minutes.

DIRECTIONS: Before the activity, visit a local library or bookseller's Web site such as Amazon (www.amazon.com). Find four books that are available in multiple editions with different covers. (For instance, classic books like *Jane Eyre,* by Charlotte Brontë, have been reprinted many times with many different covers since their first publication.) Try to select a mix of older and newer titles.

Once you've selected the four books, photocopy or print out copies of two different covers for each book. Try to choose covers with different visual styles.

Next, use tape or correction fluid to hide the titles and authors on your photocopies. (You might want to make another copy of the covers after this step, to ensure that participants won't be able to read the titles or author names.) Make sure to keep copies of the multiple covers of each book together. You should now have eight copies total—copies of two covers for Book #1, copies of two covers for Book #2, copies of two covers for Book #3, and copies of two covers for Book #4.

When participants arrive, divide them into four teams. Assign a book to each team and give it the copies of the two different covers. Give the teams the following instructions:

> **Today's activity is about appearances. In your teams, I want you to look at the two book covers I've given you and vote on which one you'd rather read, based solely on the cover. Be prepared to explain your team's decision.**

Give participants 5–10 minutes to discuss and vote. When they are finished, have each team share its decision and explanation with the larger group. Record decisions on newsprint or whiteboard. Once all four teams have presented their decisions, reveal to them that the two covers each team examined were for the same book.

DISCUSSION QUESTIONS:

1. Did any team realize that the two covers you were looking at were for the same book? Did knowing that affect your decision on which book you'd rather read? How?

2. What are the pros and cons to judging something by its appearance?

3. Have you ever witnessed a situation where someone made a judgment about a person because of how he or she looked? How did it make you feel?

44

SLOGAN CONTEST

FOCUS: Participants come up with positive slogans to promote diversity awareness in their school and community.

ADDITIONAL ASSETS: Asset 5, Caring School Climate; Asset 8, Youth as Resources; and Asset 37, Personal Power.

TIME REQUIRED: 30 – 45 minutes.

DIRECTIONS: Divide the participants into two teams, Agency A and Agency B. Give each team newsprint and markers. Share with participants the following information and instructions:

> **Advertising agencies spend billions of dollars each year creating catchy phrases and sayings to influence people to buy products. Imagine your teams are advertising agencies. Agency A is working to advertise the benefits of diversity and respect in schools, while Agency B is working to advertise the same "product" in communities. In your teams, brainstorm slogans and catchphrases that would influence people to respect and value all the different members of their school or community.**

When the teams are finished, hang their slogans around the room. Give each participant 20 stickers. They will use 10 of their stickers to vote on their favorite school slogan(s) and the other 10 to vote on their favorite community slogan(s). Participants can place their stickers on multiple slogans or use them all to vote for just one (10 maximum for a school slogan and 10 maximum for a community slogan). If you like, you can give out prizes to the people who came up with the slogans that received the most votes.

DISCUSSION QUESTIONS:

1. How easy was it to come up with sayings and slogans that encourage respect for diversity?

2. What were your favorite slogans and why?

3. So that this work is not lost, what can we do with both the school and community slogans?

4. How can these slogans be used in the school and in the community to have the most impact on people's behavior?

## 45

BACK IN TIME

FOCUS: Participants interview elders about their teenage years.

☑ LIST

You will need:

☐ a copy of the "Back in Time" handout for each participant (see page 99)

☐ notepads (one for each participant)

☐ pencils or pens

ADDITIONAL ASSETS: Asset 3, Other Adult Relationships; Asset 4, Caring Neighborhood; and Asset 14, Adult Role Models.

TIME REQUIRED: Two 45- to 60-minute meetings over one week.

DIRECTIONS: Instruct participants:

Choose an elder from your family, neighborhood, community, or faith organization. Use the questions on your "Back in Time" handouts (and additional questions you create) to interview the elder about her or his teenage experiences. The questions you create can be about lifestyles, politics, wartime, norms and expectations of the time, cultural customs, pastimes, or a combination of all the above. Set up an interview time and schedule a visit with your elder either in person or by telephone. Write up your interview so that it can be presented to the group.

Be sure to ask what it was like growing up, their most memorable experience, advice they would give a young person, a proud moment, if they ever protested and if so, for what, and any other questions you think are relevant.

After participants have completed their interviews, ask them to share their findings with the group.

DISCUSSION QUESTIONS:

1. What were some of the differences and similarities between the time period you discussed with your elder and the present?

2. How does learning about the past from one of your elders help you when it comes to diversity awareness?

3. What other benefits are there to interviewing someone from a different generation?

4. Sometimes young people and elders can have a hard time talking to one another. What are some things you could do in your community to give elders and young people more opportunities to communicate?

5. What else can you do with the information you gathered?

EDUCATIONAL EXTENSION: If time and resources are available, ask participants to create scripts from their interviews and put on a play in their school or local community center. Participants can either create a collection of short scenes from all of the interviews or focus on one particularly interesting interview.

Back in Time

1. Where were you living during this time?

2. What were some of the social "dos and don'ts" during this time?

3. What was your favorite pastime during this time? Why?

4. What major historical events do you remember from this time?

5. What was your favorite type of music/musician during this time?

6. [Create your own question]

7. [Create your own question]

8. [Create your own question]

9. [Create your own question]

10. [Create your own question]

The good things you need to succeed in life are called Developmental Assets™. This activity is designed to help you build those assets, especially Asset 34, Cultural Competence.

## 46

MYSTERY GUEST

FOCUS: Participants explore the different assumptions and stereotypes surrounding physical appearance.

ADDITIONAL ASSETS: Asset 3, Other Adult Relationships; Asset 14, Adult Role Models; and Asset 33, Interpersonal Competence.

TIME REQUIRED: 30 – 45 minutes.

DIRECTIONS: Before the activity, find a person in your community who would be willing to be interviewed by your participants. This person's appearance should in some way "trick" participants into making stereotypical judgments about her or his hobbies, job, education, physical or mental ability. (For example, you might choose a woman who works as an industrial chemist, or a 10-year-old who is a political activist.) *Note: Make sure your interview subject understands the nature of the exercise, and that he or she will initially be the subject of some stereotypical "prejudging."*

Once you've chosen a willing interview subject, bring her or him to meet with your participants. Share the following instructions:

> **Today we're lucky to have a Mystery Guest attending our activity. I want you to come up with some ideas of what our Mystery Guest is like using the five questions I'm about to read to you. I'll write down your guesses, and afterward, our Mystery Guest will reveal whether your assumptions were correct. One important ground rule: your guesses about our Mystery Guest should be honest, but respectful. Here are the questions:**
> - **What does our Mystery Guest do for a living?**
> - **What kind of music does our Mystery Guest like to listen to?**
> - **What does our Mystery Guest like to do for fun?**
> - **What does our Mystery Guest's home look like?**
> - **What is/was our Mystery Guest's favorite subject in school?**

The five questions should be written on individual sheets of newsprint. As you ask each question aloud, write participants' guesses on the appropriate piece of newsprint. When you are finished reading the questions, allow the interview subject to reveal the correct answer to each one.

DISCUSSION QUESTIONS:

1. Was it easy or hard to make guesses about a person based only on her or his appearance? Please explain.

2. Is there ever a connection between people's appearances and their personalities and characteristics? Please explain.

3. How accurate do you think opinions based on appearance are, in general?

LIST

You will need:

- ☐ an interview subject (you may choose to have two interview subjects, if available)
- ☐ newsprint and a marker

47

TAKING A STAND

FOCUS: Participants explore their beliefs about diversity and peace via famous quotations.

☑ LIST

You will need:

☐ a copy of the "Famous Quotes" list for the facilitator (see page 102)

☐ three large signs posted in the room labeled AGREE, DISAGREE, and NOT SURE

ADDITIONAL ASSETS: Asset 9, Service to Others; Asset 14, Adult Role Models; and Asset 28, Integrity.

TIME REQUIRED: 30 – 45 minutes.

DIRECTIONS: Tell participants:

I am going to read some quotes that were either said or written by a famous person. Listen carefully to the quotes. Go stand by the sign in the room that most closely represents your opinion.

Choose a quote, read it out loud, and repeat it once. Ask participants to take a stand on what they think about the quote.

Ask members of the three groups why they chose the position they did. Everyone should be able to explain her or his choice. Some quotes may call for social responsibility. Be prepared to ask participants what role they can play in making a quote a reality.

VARIATION: There are many quotes on the handout, so this activity can be done over and over again. You can also ask participants to bring in quotes of their own choosing that are related to diversity.

Famous Quotes

The real death of America will come when everyone is alike. —*James T. Ellison*

We all live with the objective of being happy; our lives are all different and yet the same. —*Anne Frank*

Diversity: the art of thinking independently together. —*Malcolm S. Forbes*

Unity and victory are synonymous. —*Samora Machel*

We have become not a melting pot but a beautiful mosaic. Different people, different beliefs, different yearnings, different hopes, different dreams. —*Jimmy Carter*

How can one not speak about war, poverty, and inequality when people who suffer from these afflictions don't have a voice to speak? —*Isabel Allende*

Human diversity makes tolerance more than a virtue; it makes it a requirement for survival. —*René Dubois*

Living on borders and in margins, keeping intact one's shifting and multiple identity and integrity, is like trying to swim in a new element, an "alien" element. —*Gloria Anzaldúa*

Ultimately, America's answer to the intolerant man is diversity, the very diversity which our heritage of religious freedom has inspired. —*Robert F. Kennedy*

Until we can understand the assumptions in which we are drenched we cannot know ourselves. —*Adrienne Rich*

There never were in the world two opinions alike, no more than two hairs or two grains; the most universal quality is diversity. —*Michel de Montaigne*

If we even tolerate any oppression of gay and lesbian Americans, if we join those who would intrude upon the choices of our hearts, then who among us shall be free? —*June Jordan*

If we cannot end now our differences, at least we can help make the world safe for diversity. —*John F. Kennedy*

If we are to achieve a richer culture, rich in contrasting values, we must recognize the whole gamut of human potentialities, and so weave a less arbitrary social fabric, one in which each diverse human gift will find a fitting place. —*Margaret Mead*

If we are to live together in peace, we must come to know each other better. —*Lyndon B. Johnson*

Insight, I believe, refers to the depth of understanding that comes by setting experiences, yours and mine, familiar and exotic, new and old, side by side, learning by letting them speak to one another. —*Mary Catherine Bateson*

If you want to make peace, you don't talk to your friends. You talk to your enemies. —*Moshe Dayan*

The longer we listen to one another—with real attention—the more commonality we will find in all our lives. That is, if we are careful to exchange with one another life stories and not simply opinions. —*Barbara Deming*

The real miracle is not to walk either on water or in thin air, but to walk on earth. —*Thich Nhat Hanh*

He who hates, hates himself. —*Zulu Proverb*

If you want to make peace with your enemy, you have to work with your enemy. Then he becomes your partner. —*Nelson Mandela*

When you find peace within yourself, you become the kind of person who can live at peace with others. —*Peace Pilgrim*

For it isn't enough to talk about peace. One must believe in it. And it isn't enough to believe in it. One must work at it. —*Eleanor Roosevelt*

Until he extends the circle of compassion to all living things, man will not himself find peace. —*Albert Schweitzer*

In all my work what I try to say is that as human beings we are more alike than we are unalike. —*Maya Angelou*

48   A PLAN OF ACTION

FOCUS: Participants create action plans for tackling a particular diversity issue in their community.

LIST

You will need:
- ☐ pencils or pens
- ☐ writing paper

ADDITIONAL ASSETS: Asset 8, Youth as Resources; Asset 9, Service to Others; and Asset 27, Equality and Social Justice.

TIME REQUIRED: 60 – 75 minutes.

DIRECTIONS: Provide participants with the following instructions:

Take 10 minutes to brainstorm social injustices that are present in your school or community. These should be issues that are important to you.

Allow participants to complete this step individually. Then, divide the group into two or three smaller teams and give instructions for the next step:

In your teams, after looking at all of the issues you brainstormed individually, choose one issue all of you would be willing to work on in order to advocate for or help create change. Then, take 10 more minutes to write down all the things the people in your team are already doing with respect to the problem, and note their thoughts and feelings about it. Next, identify what some of your challenges and barriers might be if you decided to take action. Who might oppose your plan to seek a positive solution for the injustice?

Allow participants to complete this step, then give the following instructions:

Now, use 10 more minutes to brainstorm and record potential partners who might be interested in seeing the injustice removed. Are there any individuals or groups who are already working on the problem? What progress have they made, if any? Make a list of people who might make up a partnership for change on the issue you want to work on.

Allow participants to complete this step, then give these final instructions:

Using the information you've written down, develop a plan of action. This plan should list at least two concrete steps your team can take to help erase the injustice you've chosen. Be sure to also include reasons why your actions would help eliminate the problem, the partners who might support your effort, and a list of any supplies or resources you would need to make your plan a reality.

After allowing the teams to work for at least 20 minutes on their plans, ask each team to share a few details of its plan with the group.

DISCUSSION QUESTIONS:

1. Looking at your plans, is there any way they could be put into action right now? What additional information would you need, if any, to make that possible?

2. In general, do you think it's more effective to work as a group on implementing social change, or to work alone? Why?

3. Were any parts of your plan harder to come up with than others? Why?

4. In general, what are some possible personal and societal barriers that can keep people from getting involved in issues they care about?

49 SAY IT LOUD!

FOCUS: Participants identify personal qualities and characteristics that make them proud.

☑ LIST

You will need:

☐ a copy of the "Say It Loud!" handout for each participant (see page 106)

☐ pencils or pens

ADDITIONAL ASSETS: Asset 37, Personal Power; Asset 38, Self-Esteem; and Asset 39, Sense of Purpose.

TIME REQUIRED: 20 – 45 minutes.

DIRECTIONS: Distribute the "Say It Loud!" handout. Tell participants:

Often, the message we get in society is to be something different, to "make over" ourselves, to be unhappy with who we are. Those messages appear loudly in TV advertisements and magazines. There are fewer countermessages inviting us to explore who we are and to feel proud of ourselves. Today, we want to focus on what we like about ourselves, and to share those qualities with the group. We all need to take time to affirm our positive qualities.

I want you all to think about things about yourself that make you proud. It can be your heritage, your gender, your accomplishments, your talents, your personality traits, your future aspirations, your beliefs, your values, your personal creed, and so on. Complete the "Say It Loud!" handout.

When everyone has completed the handout, collect the sheets and redistribute them. Each participant will be responsible for introducing the participant whose paper they have and reading her or his unique qualities aloud. The point is for all participants to have their accomplishments read and for everyone to applaud them for who they are and what they are most proud of. (If the group is very large, you can have the participants circle five to eight things they are most proud of as a way to save time.)

DISCUSSION QUESTIONS:

1. How easy or difficult was it to come up with 20 things you were proud of?

2. How did it feel to have someone else read all the things you are proud of?

3. How easy or difficult was it to have other group members applaud you?

4. Did any two people have the same 20 things? What does this say about this group?

5. Why do you think it is necessary to do activities like this one?

6. What can we do to continue to affirm our uniqueness every day?

Say It Loud!

Name_____

1. **Say it loud! I'm** _____ **and I'm proud!**

2. **Say it loud! I'm** _____ **and I'm proud!**

3. **Say it loud! I'm** _____ **and I'm proud!**

4. **Say it loud! I'm** _____ **and I'm proud!**

5. **Say it loud! I'm** _____ **and I'm proud!**

6. **Say it loud! I'm** _____ **and I'm proud!**

7. **Say it loud! I'm** _____ **and I'm proud!**

8. **Say it loud! I'm** _____ **and I'm proud!**

9. **Say it loud! I'm** _____ **and I'm proud!**

10. **Say it loud! I'm** _____ **and I'm proud!**

11. **Say it loud! I'm** _____ **and I'm proud!**

12. **Say it loud! I'm** _____ **and I'm proud!**

13. **Say it loud! I'm** _____ **and I'm proud!**

14. **Say it loud! I'm** _____ **and I'm proud!**

15. **Say it loud! I'm** _____ **and I'm proud!**

16. **Say it loud! I'm** _____ **and I'm proud!**

17. **Say it loud! I'm** _____ **and I'm proud!**

18. **Say it loud! I'm** _____ **and I'm proud!**

19. **Say it loud! I'm** _____ **and I'm proud!**

20. **Say it loud! I'm** _____ **and I'm proud!**

The good things you need to succeed in life are called Developmental Assets™. This activity is designed to help you build those assets, especially Asset 34, Cultural Competence.

FOCUS: Participants go beyond their social comfort zones by intentionally meeting people they would otherwise not communicate with.

You will need:

☐ Tootsie Rolls or other wrapped candies (five for each participant)

☐ index cards (five for each participant)

ADDITIONAL ASSETS: Asset 5, Caring School Climate; Asset 26, Caring; and Asset 33, Interpersonal Competence.

TIME REQUIRED: Two 30- to 45-minute meetings over one week.

DIRECTIONS: Ask participants the following questions:

- **How easy is it for you to approach a group of people you don't know very well?**
- **What are the risks in starting up a conversation with a stranger?**

Next, give each participant five Tootsie Rolls or other wrapped candy, five index cards, and the following instructions:

We are going to participate in the Tootsie Roll challenge. The goal is for us to choose people (whether at school, in your neighborhood, or in your congregation) with whom we normally don't have contact, but who we're interested in getting to know better. The challenge is to engage this person in a conversation. You must share something about yourself, and they must share something about themselves. At the end of the short conversation, you must give this person one of your Tootsie Rolls. On one of your cards, write their name and what you learned about them. At the end of the week, you should have no Tootsie Rolls left from your original supply, and five completed index cards.

Challenge yourselves to go beyond your usual boundaries.

During your second meeting, ask participants to share their experiences using the discussion questions below.

DISCUSSION QUESTIONS:

1. How did you choose people to talk to for this activity?
2. How receptive were people to having a brief conversation with you?
3. If you were approached and given a Tootsie Roll, how did that make you feel?
4. Did anything about doing this activity surprise you?
5. What do you think was the point of the Tootsie Roll Challenge?
6. What are some things you learned about yourself in doing this challenge?
7. Will you continue to get to know the people with whom you shared Tootsie Rolls? Why or why not?

Facilitator Notes

Facilitator Notes

Facilitator Notes

Facilitator Notes

Additional Search Institute Resources

Attitudes and Behaviors (A&B): The Developmental Assets Survey for Grades 6–12. This 156-item survey provides an aggregate portrait of the 40 Developmental Assets as experienced by your 6th- through 12th-grade youth. In addition to measuring Developmental Assets, the survey also measures eight thriving indicators, five developmental deficits, and 24 risk-taking behaviors.

"Ask Me Where I'm Going" and Other Revealing Messages from Today's Teens. This intimate little book will touch your heart as you read poignant and practical "real words" from teens describing what they really want from the caring adults in their lives.

Building Assets Together: 135 Group Activities for Helping Youth Succeed, by Jolene L. Roehlkepartain. Use any of these fabulous, fun activities and worksheets with young people, and in less than 30 minutes, the power of positive energy will ripple throughout the room. Creative, interesting, and thought provoking, these activities will produce laughter, insight, and more successful young people. It includes 94 interactive group activities for 6th- through 12th-grade youth, plus 41 attractive, reproducible worksheets that help youth understand their own assets.

Conversations on the Go: Clever Questions to Keep Teens and Grown-Ups Talking by Mary Ackerman. This stimulating, go-anywhere book gives teens and adults a chance to find out what the other one

thinks. Filled with intriguing questions, some deep and some just fun, it's guaranteed to stretch the imagination and bring out each other's personality and true self.

Life Freaks Me Out — And Then I Deal with It by K. L. Hong. *Turbulent. Exhilarating. Confusing. Real.* These words describe what **Life Freaks Me Out** is all about—living, being, and growing up as a teen. This down-to-earth memoir touches on hard-hitting issues—drugs, alcohol, self-esteem, relationships, sex—to emphasize to today's teens the power of choice, and the importance of finding their own values and truths as they grow up.

More Building Assets Together: 130 Group Activities for Helping Youth Succeed, by Rebecca Grothe. We created a batch of great youth activities, shared them with the world in **Building Assets Together,** and pretty soon were flooded with ideas for more great activities. This volume is filled with 130 challenging and fun activities to engage youth, including "Block Party," "Tell the Press," and the "Ultimate Homework Hangout."

Tag, You're It! 50 Easy Ways to Connect with Young People by Kathleen Kimball-Baker. This motivating book offers commonsense ideas to connect and build assets with young people. Youth workers, parents, educators, businesspeople, congregation leaders, and anyone who cares about youth will love this book. The **Tag, You're It!** card deck and the **Tag, You're It!** posters are also specifically designed to spark conversations between youth and adults.